MICHIEL R. LEENDERS
LOUISE A. MAUFFETTE-LEENDERS
JAMES A. ERSKINE

writing cases

fourth edition

Richard Ivey School of Business
The University of Western Ontario

Ivey

Writing Cases
Fourth Edition

ISBN   0-7714-2270-9

The earlier editions of this book were published under the title
Case Research: The Case Writing Process

Copyright © 1973, 1978, 1989, 2001, 2010 Richard Ivey School of Business

This book may be ordered from:

   Ivey Publishing
   Richard Ivey School of Business
   The University of Western Ontario
   London, Ontario, Canada, N6A 3K7

   Phone: (+1) 519-661-3208
   Fax: (+1) 519-661-3882
   E-mail: cases@ivey.uwo.ca
   Web Site: http://www.ivey.uwo.ca/cases
                   http://www.ivey.uwo.ca/workshops

Printed in Canada by Senton Printing, London, Ontario. No part of this publication may be reproduced without the prior written permission of the copyright holder.

about the authors

The author team has collectively taught case learning, writing and teaching workshops to more than 15,000 participants in over 60 countries on all continents.

Michiel R. Leenders is Professor Emeritus and the former Leenders Purchasing Management Association of Canada Chair at the Richard Ivey School of Business. He received a degree in Mining Engineering from the University of Alberta, an MBA from The University of Western Ontario and his doctorate from the Harvard Business School. He is a former director of the School's Ph.D. program and teaches and consults internationally. Mike's texts have been translated into ten languages. He has authored and co-authored ten books in supply management. Mike received the Leaders in Management Education Award sponsored by the Financial Post and Bell Canada and is a director of the ING Bank of Canada.

Louise A. Mauffette-Leenders holds a BA from Collège Jean-de-Brébeuf, a BBA and MBA from l'École des Hautes Études Commerciales of Montréal, Québec. As case writer and research associate at The Richard Ivey School of Business at The University of Western Ontario, she wrote dozens of cases in all areas of management, including the non-profit sector. Louise has worked extensively in the social services and international development. She has written and taught cases in various training programs for social service providers.

James A. Erskine is Professor Emeritus and taught Operations Management at the Richard Ivey School of Business with a special interest in the human in the system. He has Engineering and MBA degrees from The University of Western Ontario and a doctorate from Indiana University. Jim has served as Dean at the Lahore University of Management Sciences in Pakistan and is a past chairperson of the Honors Undergraduate Business Program at Ivey. He has been cited for distinguished contribution by both the World Association for Case Method Research and Application (WACRA) and the North American Case Research Association (NACRA). Jim is a 3-M teaching fellow recognizing him as one of Canada's best university professors.

acknowledgements

Everyone who has ever written a textbook knows that such an effort requires the assistance of a large number of people.

As co-authors we have slowly, and at times painfully, learned how to use each other's strengths and experiences to forge a common document all three of us believe represents our very best efforts.

Our mentors go back a long way to many individuals at many educational institutions, with the Harvard Business School and The Richard Ivey School of Business as two key sources. Clearly, Professors Andrew R. Towl and C. Roland Christensen at Harvard were two giants who set us off in the right direction. We have interviewed hundreds of others and enjoyed the writings of various colleagues who shared their expertise in notes, lectures, articles and books over the years.

The thousands of case writers, case teachers and students who have participated in our workshops and classes have been invaluable sources of suggestions as we tested our ideas on them. For the last three decades we have been on a learning curve with the assistance of so many to push us along.

Sharon Rochard, Elaine Carson, Sue LeMoine and Beth Sinclair have found various ways of translating our ideas into graphically acceptable form. Jackie Watson-Palmer's experienced case writing eyes scanned the final document before Senton Printing with Jake Thain, Candace Dorward and a host of capable experts managed to put it all into book form.

We acknowledge the warm support of Ivey Publishing.

preface

This text is about writing good cases quickly. This fourth edition is a substantial departure from the third in that it identifies case writing as a three phase process and guides the reader through each phase. From the first edition in 1973, we have tried to apply operations management principles to the process of case writing to focus on producing good quality cases quickly. By concentrating on both efficiency and effectiveness, we developed a number of tools and concepts to reduce set-up time and to assure quality. New ideas in this edition include the Case Origin Grid, the Case Shopping List, action triggers and the story line and decision frame cuts. Another addition is the class testing of the new case.

We still believe the development of the Case Plan with its five components is the central planning tool for effective case development.

This book is accompanied by our *Learning with Cases* text because cases are written to help students learn. We also believe that the serious case writer should be fully familiar with our third book, *Teaching with Cases*.

All of the material contained in this text has been fully tested in over 60 countries on all continents with thousands of workshop participants representing many disciplines. We are confident, therefore, that the new case writer who faithfully follows the three phase process of case writing advocated in this text can produce good cases fast.

As the case method attracts increasing attention as an effective participative approach to education, the need for new and exciting cases is growing all over the world. This trend requires a supply of well-trained case writers, and *Writing Cases* is their guide.

contents

CHAPTER 1: INTRODUCTION 1
What Is the Case Method? 1
What Is a Case? 3
Why Use Cases? 5
Why Write Cases? 7
Learning to Write Cases 8
Terminology 10
Organization and Presentation of the Material. 11

CHAPTER 2: CONCEPTS, TOOLS AND PROCESS 13
Key Challenges in Effective Case Writing 13
    Objectives 13
    Communication 15
The Case Difficulty Cube 17
    The Analytical Dimension 18
    The Conceptual Dimension 19
    The Presentation Dimension 20
    The Combination of the Three Dimensions 22
The Case Plan 24
The Three Phase Case Writing Process 25
    Phase 1 25
    Phase 2 28
    Phase 3 29

CHAPTER 3: ORIGIN, LEAD, INITIAL CONTACT 31
Case Origin 31
    The Need to Write a Case 31
    The Kind of Case to Write 33
    The Case Origin Grid 37
Case Leads 42
    Types of Case Leads 42
    Finding an Appropriate Lead 43
Initial Contact 44
    Arranging the Initial Appointment 45
    Preparing for the First Interview 46
    The Case Shopping List 50
    The First Interview 52

CHAPTER 4: CASE FOCUS CHOICES AND DISGUISE 57
Case Focus Choices 57
   1. The Choice of Issue. 57
   2. The Choice of Timing. 57
      Action Triggers 63
   3. The Choice of Decision Maker or Focal Person 66
Disguise. 66
   Disguise of Information 67
   Disguise Approach 69

CHAPTER 5: CASE PLAN AND PROVISIONAL
               RELEASE 71
The Case Plan. 71
   1. The Opening Paragraph. 72
   2. The Brief Statement of Teaching Objectives 82
   3. The Proposed Organization or
      Outline of the Case by Subtitles. 84
   4. The Data Requirements List 87
   5. The Time Plan 94
Provisional Release 95

CHAPTER 6: DATA COLLECTION 99
The Personal Interview. 100
   Preparation. 100
   Interviewing Rules 101
   Note Taking 104
   Recording and Videotaping. 104
   Collecting Other Materials 105
   Subsequent Data Gathering. 105
Data Collection Pitfalls and Difficulties. 105
   Questionable Reliability and Validity of Data 106
   Unpredictable Factors 107
   Uncooperative Interviewee 108
   Inappropriate Roles for the Case Writer 108
Data Security and Confidentiality 109
Data Organization. 109

CHAPTER 7: CASE WRITING AND
               PRELIMINARY TEACHING NOTE. 111
Writing a Rough Draft. 111
   Rough Drafting Conventions 113

Preparing a Preliminary Teaching Note................ 117
    Case Title 117
    Opening Paragraph................................ 117
    Teaching Objectives................................ 118
    Immediate Issue(s) 118
    Basic Issue(s) 118
    Suggested Student Assignment 119
    Case Analysis..................................... 119
Revising the Rough Draft............................. 120
Editing the Case..................................... 121
    The Nine C's Case Editing Checklist................ 121

CHAPTER 8: RELEASE 129
Release Purposes 129
    1. Release Assures Academic Honesty 129
    2. Release Authenticates the Data................... 129
    3. Release Grants Permission to Use the Case 130
    4. Release Maintains Positive Relations.............. 130
Tasks for Obtaining Release........................... 130
    Release Request................................... 131
    Follow-up.. 134
    Correcting and Filing 134
    Registration 134
Kinds of Release..................................... 136
    Traditional Release 136
    Restricted Release 136
    Multiple Release 136
    Delayed Release 137
    Re-release 137
    Release Not Required 137

CHAPTER 9: TEACHING NOTE AND CLASS TEST .. 139
The Teaching Note................................... 139
    Suggested Additional Reading/Data Gathering 141
    Possible Teaching Aids............................. 141
    Discussion Questions for Use in Class 141
    Additional Points to Raise.......................... 141
    Teaching Suggestions 142
    The Case Teaching Plan 142

Class Test. 144
    The Need for Class Testing 145
    Kinds of Class Test 146
    What Needs Testing 147
    Interpreting Class Test Results 149
Case Revisions and Re-release. 151
    Teachers Who Are Not Authors That Wish to Make
        Changes to Cases. 152

CHAPTER 10: OTHER CONSIDERATIONS. 155
Case Length 155
Case Life and Updating Old Cases. 156
    Case Life and Turnover Rate. 156
    Revision and Updating 157
Case Writing and Consulting. 157
Academic Credit for Case Writing 158
    1. Is Case Writing Worthy of Academic Credit?. 158
    2. Is a Case a Publication? 159
    3. Is Case Writing a Research or
       Teaching Materials Development Activity? 160
Using Others to Write Cases 161
    Selection 161
    Training. 162
    Supervision 163
    Students as Case Writers 164
Case Costs and Financing 165
Others Forms of Cases 166
    International Cases 166
    Series Cases 168
    Research Cases. 169
    In-house Cases. 169
    Multimedia Cases 170
Conclusion 171

APPENDIXES 173
Appendix 1: Description of the Case Writing Process. 173
Appendix 2: Sample Case 175
Appendix 3: Sample Preliminary Teaching Note 179
Appendix 4: Major Case Distribution Centers of the World . 184

INDEX. 186

CHAPTER ONE

introduction

This book is about writing good cases fast. The focus is on writing field-based decision-oriented cases for educational purposes. This text is the outcome of our collective efforts to make the case writing process more efficient and effective. It provides guidance to anyone wishing to write a case. This fourth edition complements the latest editions of *Teaching with Cases* and *Learning with Cases*.

WHAT IS THE CASE METHOD?

The case method is a discussion-based learning methodology that enables participants, through the use of cases, to learn by doing and by teaching others. A case is a description of an actual issue faced by a person in an organization. The repetitive opportunity to identify, analyze and solve a number of cases in a variety of settings prepares learners to become truly professional in their field of work.

Although cases have been used in one form or another by both law and medicine for a long period, the case method as used in the teaching of management is relatively new. The Harvard Business School is credited for its innovative role in business education. In 1910, Dr. Copeland was advised by Dean Gay to use student discussion in addition to lectures. From 1909 to 1919, business executives came to classes to present problems, and students were asked to write analyses and recommendations. The first book of written cases was published in 1921 by Dr. Copeland after the prodding from a new Dean, Wallace B. Donham. Dean Donham, a lawyer trained by the case method, saw the importance of using cases in administrative settings and pushed hard to get a total school commitment to the case method.

In 1919, two classics scholars at The University of Western Ontario (U. W. O.) in London, Canada, Dr. W. Sherwood Fox, Dean of Arts and Science, and Dr. K. P. R. Neville, Registrar, had the vision to initiate the teaching of business based on the Harvard case method. After carefully reviewing all recognized business courses of university level in North America, they concluded that the course given at the Harvard School of Business appeared to offer the soundest of all methods under scrutiny. In 1922, they hired Ellis H. Morrow, a Harvard graduate, to launch a Canadian version of the Harvard program. Today, the Richard Ivey School of Business at U. W. O. is a leader in case method management education on a national and international level and the second largest producer of cases in the world.

Over the years and through the various disciplines that have adopted it, the case method has come to mean different things to different people. All under the same appellation, educators include different teaching styles, techniques and activities. While it is out of the scope of this book to discuss these variances, it is important, nevertheless, to articulate briefly what the authors believe are the main tenets of the "case method," as they relate to teaching and learning with cases.

Learning with cases is a three stage process involving individual preparation, small group discussion and large group or class discussion. Each stage is crucial and contributes in different ways to the quality and quantity of learning in a progressive and cumulative fashion. Our book *Learning with Cases* shows how to work effectively in each of these three stages.

Cases give students and instructors the same information from which decisions are to be made. From this starting point, each will obviously play a distinctly different role in the process of learning. Exhibit 1-1 summarizes the teacher and student roles in a regular case class.

Exhibit 1-1
THE TEACHER AND STUDENT ROLES IN A REGULAR CASE CLASS

When	Teacher	Student or Participant
Before Class	Assigns case and often readings	Receives case and assignment
	Prepares for class	Prepares individually
	May consult colleagues	Discusses case in small group
During Class	Deals with readings	Raises questions regarding readings
	Leads case discussion	Participates in discussion
After Class	Evaluates and records student participation	Compares personal analysis with colleagues' analyses
	Evaluates materials and updates teaching note	Reviews class discussion for major concepts learned

WHAT IS A CASE?

A case is a description of an actual situation, commonly involving a decision, a challenge, an opportunity, a problem or an issue faced by a person or persons in an organization. The case requires the reader to step figuratively into the position of a particular decision maker.

Cases normally appear in print form. Increasingly, cases are also presented in other formats such as film, video tape, CD ROM, audio tape, disk, or a combination of these. With interactive computer graphics, communications networks and hypermedia databases, cases can engage participants in novel ways. However, hard copy cases currently remain the most common type because of cost and convenience. The prime focus of *Writing Cases* is on the traditional type of case.

Cases are field-based. The source of every case rests with the individual in an organization who was involved in a decision or problem. A case researcher visits the organization and collects the data that comprise the case.

Cases are released. Someone in the organization signs an official release document giving permission to use the case for educational purposes. Chapter 8 will cover at length the purposes of the release, related tasks associated with it and its variations. It is this release that truly distinguishes cases from any other kind of educational material.

A case is the product of a carefully thought-out research and reporting process. The content of a case varies with the educational purpose. Following specific teaching objectives, the case researcher reports the information about the decision faced by the focal person of the case. Certain aspects of the situation or decision may be highlighted, while others are underplayed or deleted.

Ultimately, a new case is tested in the classroom, as its final assessment lies in its application. Did the case accomplish the educational purpose intended?

Other educational materials such as an exercise, a problem, an article or a simulation may make excellent teaching materials. However, they are different from a case in that the writer or author may not have used real life data and obtained a release. Sometimes these materials are improperly referred to as cases and occasionally bear the label of "armchair" cases, implying they were written from the security of one's office in a comfortable armchair.

The source, the collection process and subsequent release provide the key distinctions between a "real" case and an "armchair" case. Why is this distinction important? The success of the case method is totally dependent upon the student's willingness and ability to identify with the decision maker's position and the data given. The student takes the case writer's word for it that a "Mr. Park" or "Ms. Lee" really existed and that the case material was based on a true situation. The moment the student starts doubting the reality of the situation described, his or her ability to give the case full attention and to take the task seriously diminishes. Academic honesty requires disclosure of the source of data and the research methodology used.

WHY USE CASES?

Cases permit participants to learn by doing and teaching others. They allow students to take on the roles and responsibilities of specific people in specific organizations. It is a form of on-the-job training. The case method provides an opportunity to become deeply involved in decisions actually faced by real people in real organizations; to take ownership, to feel the pressure, to recognize the risks, and to expose one's ideas to those of others.

Cases allow students to accumulate experience while addressing issues across a wide range of functional areas, levels of responsibilities, types and sizes of organizations and industries, as well as locations throughout the world. It is the cumulative impact of these different case challenges that will permit students to take on future tasks knowing that the process of tackling decisions effectively has become a major personal asset.

Cases give students a chance to practice the art as well as the science of management in a laboratory setting, with little corporate and personal risk involved. In essence, cases are to management students what cadavers are to medical students – the opportunity to practice on the real thing harmlessly.

Cases are also an excellent tool to test the understanding of theory and to develop theoretical insights. Cases themselves may contain theoretical materials or readings may be assigned in conjunction with cases to cover theoretical perspectives. Cases provide an opportunity to see how theory applies in practice or to identify the need for theory.

Cases provide information about how work is planned and organized in various settings, how systems operate and how organizations compete. The case method of instruction is particularly well-suited to deal with new and complex situations. Managers need to adapt to ever-changing circumstances.

Cases force students to make decisions with available information and to specify missing information. Managers seldom have access to all the information pertinent to decisions.

Cases help students develop self-confidence, the ability to think independently and work cooperatively with peers. Moreover, cases foster the development of insights into personal strengths and weaknesses and allow for profound personal growth. Cases oblige students to take responsibility for their own learning.

Cases engage students in a process of learning how to learn. While every case is different, it is the process of learning how to learn that is generalizable.

Cases provide the opportunity to develop a wide range of skills, as summarized in Exhibit 1-2.

Lastly, learning with cases is fun.

Exhibit 1-2
INVENTORY OF SKILLS
DEVELOPED BY THE CASE METHOD

1. **Qualitative and quantitative analytical skills,** including problem identification skills, data handling skills and critical thinking skills

2. **Decision making skills,** including generating different alternatives, selecting decision criteria, evaluating alternatives, choosing the best one, and formulating congruent action and implementation plans

3. **Application skills,** using various tools, techniques and theories

4. **Oral communication skills,** including speaking, listening and debating skills

5. **Time management skills,** dealing with individual preparation, small group discussion and class discussion

6. **Interpersonal or social skills,** dealing with peers, solving conflicts and practicing the art of compromise, in small or large groups

7. **Creative skills,** looking for and finding solutions geared to the unique circumstances of each case

8. **Written communication skills**, involving regular and effective note-taking, case reports and case exams

WHY WRITE CASES?

Keeping pace with change is not only one of the real opportunities, but also one of the challenges, of the case method. New cases are as essential to the case method as new blood to a donor clinic. There are many reasons for the continuing development of new cases. The most obvious is that existing cases become obsolete. With the passage of time, each case will become outdated. The management principles contained in it may last forever, but its context becomes outdated. Student and faculty interest can be maintained primarily with current material, as management theories and practices are in constant evolution.

Students are always concerned with the relevance of the material used. They want cases that address today's problems and decisions in their intended place of work. Students are quick to point out that popular courses are those with a high percentage of current cases from their own country. Cases will be relevant if they are set in the environment where the students are living and will be working. A case involving the marketing of snowshoes in Finland will be of limited appeal to Brazilian students. Students prefer cases in which they can readily identify with the key person in the case.

The faculty member, instructor or trainer also needs relevant cases. In course or program planning prior to class, the educator has the responsibility of selecting the material to be taught. The educator can select cases from those written by others or may decide to write one. If the teacher has confidence in the case material, he or she can better concentrate on the case discussion facilitating task. One of the best ways to achieve this confidence is to write one's own cases. Teaching a class fully armed with the live facts of the case situation not only assists the teacher, but also increases students' excitement. In turn, having experience writing one's own cases, the teacher may be better able to use material developed by others.

LEARNING TO WRITE CASES

It used to be that most people who knew how to write cases had learned the hard way. "You sink or swim." Many were convinced that it was the only way to learn, and as long as there was little demand for cases and the use of cases was largely restricted to a few North American schools, "sink or swim" was perhaps acceptable. However, these case writers would seldom talk about their filing cabinet full of unreleased and therefore unusable cases, or the time and money it took to write them.

These days are largely over. Since the first edition of this book in 1973, thousands of educators across the world have read about the state-of-the-art in case writing or participated in workshops such as the annual case writing workshop at the Richard Ivey School of Business at The University of Western Ontario. They have adopted the various tools and concepts to facilitate the case writing process that we have developed and refined over the years.

Nevertheless, case writing often remains an individual activity where the teacher performs all stages of the work. The individual nature of the case writing task, on the whole, precludes the sharing of information among colleagues. Some teachers use their students to develop new cases; others have the resources to employ one or two assistants. These students or assistants seldom have prior case writing experience. Their training is done (or not done) by the teacher who takes on a supervisory role. Assistants seldom stay full-time case writers for longer than one year, although they may continue in academic life and eventually become teachers themselves. This apprenticeship system is still common. The high turnover of apprentices results in a continuing training task for the supervisor.

It is not possible to avoid the apprentice system completely. Assistants play a useful role in the case development process. It is not necessary, however, for each assistant or newcomer to case writing to obtain all guidance from one person. Current knowledge can be shared by many. The Internet now provides various forums to discuss case writing activities.

Whether a particular case needs to be written is an individual decision. How it is to be written and how it is to be used are also largely individual decisions. Hopefully, these decisions should be based on a reasonable understanding of what alternatives are available. To help case writers achieve and share this understanding is the purpose of this book.

TERMINOLOGY

Case writing, case development, case research, and writing cases are terms used interchangeably. All denote the full process from the decision to use and write a case, developing leads, initial company contact, data collection, writing and release, to classroom test and teaching note.

A *case writer* is anyone writing a case. A case writer may be an educator, teacher, instructor, student, trainer, manager or researcher. A case writer working for someone who teaches is often called a research assistant or research associate. In this context, research assistant, research associate and case writer are synonymous terms.

The *contact person* in the case writing process is sometimes called the case lead. This person may or may not be the focal person of the case.

The *focal person* of the case may also be called key person or decision maker.

A *teacher*, trainer, instructor, educator, professor or faculty member is someone responsible for the teaching of a class, a seminar, a workshop, a course or a program.

A *student* denotes a participant, case reader or any person engaged in the case learning process.

The word *decision* is often used to describe an issue, challenge, problem or opportunity faced by the key person in the case. The decision may also be a recommendation on how to solve the case.

A *course*, seminar, workshop, training session or program is an educational activity within which the use of a case may be considered desirable.

ORGANIZATION AND PRESENTATION OF THE MATERIAL

This text starts with the presentation of the concepts, tools and the process that we have developed to facilitate case writing. Therefore, Chapter 2 introduces the Case Plan, the Case Difficulty Cube, and the proposed three phase case writing process.

The seven subsequent chapters cover the chronological steps of case development: case origin, lead and initial contact in Chapter 3; case focus choices and disguise in Chapter 4; detailed Case Plan and provisional release in Chapter 5; data collection in Chapter 6; writing process, including rough draft, preliminary teaching note and editing of the case in Chapter 7; release in Chapter 8; completion of the teaching note and testing of a new case in class in Chapter 9.

Chapter 10 presents additional considerations, including case length, case life and updating old cases, case writing and consulting, academic credit for case writing, using others to write cases, case costs and financing, and different case formats.

Extensive experience with this text in training thousands of people to write cases has shown its usefulness. The new case writer can get started more quickly on the case writing process and produce good cases faster. The accomplished practitioner can use this text to train assistants and save valuable personal time. Anyone can use this text as a self-teaching device on how to write cases.

CHAPTER TWO

concepts, tools and process

This chapter will first review the key challenges in effective case writing. Then it will introduce the concepts of the Case Difficulty Cube and the Case Plan. It will close with an overview of the three phase case writing process.

KEY CHALLENGES IN EFFECTIVE CASE WRITING

There are two major challenges to case writing effectiveness: 1) inadequately defined objectives; and 2) communication problems between the educator, the case writer (if different from the educator) and the contact person in the contributing organization.

Objectives

Case writing effectiveness may be assessed against five main objectives: quality, quantity, cost, timeliness and continuity. Each is important in its own right and also in relation to each other.

Quality

Case quality has several dimensions. First and foremost, case quality relates to the usefulness of the case produced in relation to the educational objectives sought. Does it work, or will it work, in the classroom as intended? Does it meet its educational objectives fully or only marginally?

Part of case quality, as perceived by its reader, is the assurance that the case is original and based on carefully researched data.

Furthermore, the finished case, if it is well presented and well edited, will represent a certain quality standard apart from its content. Quality, therefore, is composed of three main sub-areas: the ability to perform the educational objectives sought; the quality of the data and research method used; and the quality of presentation of the final product.

The interesting aspect of quality in terms of educational objectives is that it is primarily dependent on the choice of issue and the plan for the case format and content. Our experience shows that at least sixty percent of this quality dimension is determined in the first ten percent of case writing time spent.

Quantity

Quantity relates to the productivity of the case writer. What if someone produced one good case, but it took two years to write? Obviously, there must be concern with quantity produced for the time and resources spent. General experience shows that without a quantity objective, case writers are likely to have a low output. While quantity depends, of course, on various factors, the rule of thumb for a case of 10 to 15 pages plus exhibits has been one case a month. However, excellent short cases of less than five pages can be written in less than a week.

Cost

Cost is also a significant factor in assessing case writing effectiveness. Obvious case writing costs include salaries and travel. Where case writing is part of someone's academic activities, some kind of allocation to represent time spent may be used. The time of other personnel, including resources in the contributing organization, should also be considered.

In setting cost objectives, the case researcher should at least consider marginal time and expense attributable to planned case writing activities. Normally, these would be educational resources that require budgeting.

Timeliness

On-time completion or delivery is another measure of effectiveness. The impact of on-time performance on the relationships of all parties involved in case writing is frequently underestimated.

Traditionally, the large number of uncertainties involved in case development have made completion date forecasting difficult. Variables include availability and access to data and personnel in the contributing organization, supervisory attention and the number of drafts required.

Continuity

Continuity recognizes that a fine case produced quickly at the cost of an institutional or organizational upset is not worth the price. The need for maintaining the image of the institution seeking the material and for strengthening business-academic ties is very important. It should be possible to make an assessment at the end of a case writing project regarding the impact on the managers involved in the contributing organization. Were they impressed, disappointed, surprised, neutral, negative or positive? Did the case writer explicitly set good relations as a target inherent in the research activity?

Communication

The second major challenge to case writing effectiveness relates to communication between instructor, case writer (if different from the instructor), and the contact person in the contributing organization. The teaching/learning process itself and the development of learning materials are both heavily dependent on the quality of the communications involved. The educator has a set of learning objectives for the student group enrolled in a specific course, seminar, workshop or program and has the responsibility to choose or develop the appropriate materials for this task.

A thorny problem in supervisor-case writer communications is their mutual understanding of the task ahead and the specific case writing objectives involved. If the supervisor is not explicit, the case writer may substitute his or her own assumptions and objectives. For example, the case writer often feels that the length of the case reflects the amount of work that has been done. Similarly, a case written to make the main issue indiscernible from other minor issues must be a tribute to its astute author. The more difficult the final case seems, the smarter the case writer must be. The end result of such a misunderstanding may well be a case of little or no use to the educator.

The other dimension of the communication process involves the educator and the personnel in the contributing organization. How does the educator convey to the contact person in the contributing organization what the educational objectives are? How can the educator effectively communicate what he or she is trying to do, and learn in turn from the organization what it can provide?

In the absence of any comments to the contrary, the manager in the contributing organization often assumes that the final case presentation and format will be flattering. The manager may also feel that certain aspects should be heavily weighted, others ignored. Confronted with a finished product bearing little resemblance to earlier expectations, the manager may well refuse to sign a release form, or sign reluctantly and secretly vow never to get involved again. Neither result is acceptable to a good case writer. The Case Difficulty Cube, the Case Plan and the three phase process have proved their worth in addressing these two major challenges to case writing effectiveness.

THE CASE DIFFICULTY CUBE

Every case represents a certain set of tasks for its reader. For the student who will have to read and analyze the case, the level of difficulty will normally dictate the amount of time which needs to be spent to master the material. Since student time is always limited, it behooves the educator to have an understanding of the difficulty of the case material used. The degree of difficulty, or the educational challenge in the case, can be viewed as having three major dimensions: analytical, conceptual and presentation. In Exhibit 2-1 the analytical dimension is the X axis, the conceptual dimension the Y axis and the presentation dimension the Z axis. Three degrees of difficulty have been assigned to each dimension.

Exhibit 2-1
THE THREE DIMENSIONS OF CASE DIFFICULTY

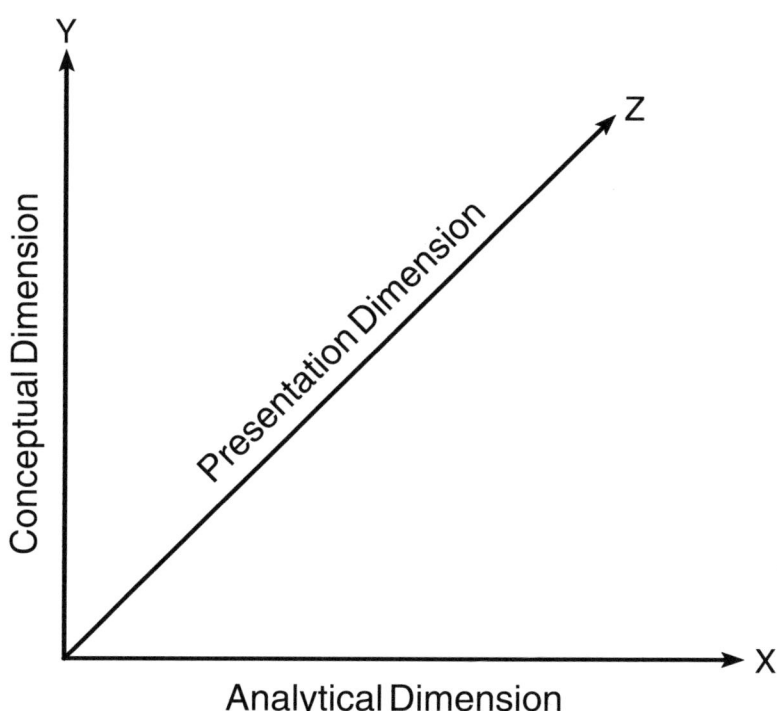

The Analytical Dimension

The analytical dimension of a case raises the question, "What is the case reader's task with respect to the key decision or issue of the case?" The analytical task depends on how the decision is presented in the case.

The case may be written with the issue stated, plus the alternatives considered, the decision criteria used and the final decision taken. For example, "Susan Lee, the finance manager of Excelsior Inc., was seeking additional funds for an expansion project and, after considering debt and equity options, decided that borrowing the money was the best decision." The participant's task becomes to assess whether the decision taken was, indeed, appropriate and the process followed correct, whether further alternatives or decision criteria might have been considered and what the future consequences could be.

This kind of case has an analytical difficulty degree of one. In other words, the participant's task is about as easy as it can get on the analytical dimension. By the way, these cases tend to be dull. Most participants in the case learning process recognize that by the time they get a chance to study a case, the situation described in the case has probably been decided in real life. Nevertheless, there is a difference between realizing this and being told so in the case. It is a bit difficult to work assiduously on these "one degree of analytical difficulty" cases when you have already been given the final decision actually taken.

A case may be written about exactly the same issue, either with or without some alternatives provided, but excluding the final decision taken. This type of case is the second degree of analytical difficulty, the one most commonly encountered in cases. Using the example of Ms. Lee above, two ways the case could be presented follow: "Ms. Lee, the finance manager at Excelsior Inc., was seeking additional funds for an expansion project and wanted to determine whether debt or equity financing would be the best way to secure new capital." Or, "Ms. Lee, the finance manager at Excelsior Inc., was seeking additional funds for an expansion project and wanted to determine the best way to secure new capital." The participant's task now becomes to analyze the situation, generate alternatives, evaluate the alternatives against specified decision criteria, make a decision, and develop an action and implementation plan.

A case moves to the third degree of analytical difficulty when even the decision that needs to be made is not identified. There is only a description of a situation. For example, "Ms. Lee, finance manager of Excelsior Inc., was reviewing the corporation's current financial position." Now the participant's task becomes to analyze the situation, figure out whether a decision needs to be taken and what alternatives might be considered, what decision criteria should be applied, which alternative is preferable, how it might be implemented and what the outcomes are likely to be. This third degree of analytical difficulty is obviously the most challenging.

Thus, the way the case writer frames the decision in the case represents different degrees of analytical difficulty for the participant and affects the amount of time required to complete the analytical task.

The Conceptual Dimension

The conceptual or theoretical dimension of the case is concerned with the question, "What theories, concepts or techniques might be useful in the understanding and/or resolution of this case situation?"

Concepts or theoretical perspectives may be contained in chapters or article readings assigned with the case, or in the case itself. They may also have been covered earlier in the course or in other courses. Or they may come after the case, once the necessity for the theoretical perspective is established through the case. At the time of course design, the educator made a decision how best to integrate the concepts or theory in a practical sense using a case. Cases often present and illustrate more concepts, theories or techniques than most people realize.

Like the analytical dimension, the conceptual dimension of the case is divided into three degrees of difficulty. Difficulty in a conceptual sense has two aspects. First, how difficult is the concept or theory in or of itself? Can someone new to this idea understand it from just carefully reading about it in a textbook or an article without further class explanation? If so, this concept is simple and assigned the first degree of difficulty. Second, conceptual difficulty relates to the number of concepts to be used simultaneously to address the decision(s) or issue(s) on which the case is focused. One or two simple concepts constitute a difficulty degree of one.

One can easily see what increases the degree of conceptual difficulty in a case. The simple concept becomes complex, requiring extensive and repeated discussion and explanation in class, sometimes to the extent of lectures and/or problems or exercises. The single concept becomes many. Integrative courses, requiring a variety of other prerequisite courses and theoretical material, tend to use cases with a high level of conceptual difficulty.

Conceptual difficulty is a relative notion. What may be difficult for one person may not be that difficult for someone else who is either particularly adept at grasping a certain concept or may have learned it earlier. Therefore it is the educator's judgment what the conceptual difficulty of a case is for the average member of a learning group or a class.

The Presentation Dimension

The third educational challenge in a case relates to the presentation dimension which provides an opportunity to develop skills in sorting and structuring information. It raises the question, "What is really important and relevant information here and what is still missing?"

The presentation dimension is also divided into three degrees of difficulty. At the first degree of difficulty the case:

1. is short;
2. is well-organized;
3. contains almost all relevant information;
4. contains little extraneous information; and
5. is conveyed in a single, simple format, most often written.

Such a case can be read quickly and relevant information is accessed easily. Actually, one of the criticisms of the case method is exactly on this point. The argument is that in real life problems and decisions do not come to the decision maker in such a nice, clean, well-organized fashion. Actually, cases low in presentation difficulty are very useful for educational purposes, since they allow concentration on the other two dimensions of case difficulty without burdening students with a massive presentation challenge.

One can easily see that the degree of difficulty related to the presentation of the case can be increased by changing up to all five of the previously mentioned points. Thus:

1. short becomes long;
2. well-organized becomes disorganized;
3. available relevant information becomes missing relevant information;
4. little extraneous information becomes a lot of extraneous information; and
5. a single format, probably written, becomes multiple formats such as written, plus video, plus database, etc.

The greater the degree of difficulty on the presentation dimension, the longer the participant needs to spend on reading, sorting, prioritizing, identifying missing information, and organizing and structuring data.

The Combination of the Three Dimensions

Three degrees of difficulty along each of the three axes create a cube containing 27 sub-cubes (see Exhibit 2-2). Thus a (3,3,3) case is one where the learner will be challenged to identify the problem; may have difficulty understanding the concepts or theories which need to be used; and will encounter additional difficulty because the case is long, with a lot of extraneous information and, possibly, not clearly presented.

In contrast, a (1,1,1) case is simple and straight-forward on each dimension. It identifies the problem and a solution, is simple in concept, and contains relevant, clearly presented material. Low level difficulty cases are often written for the introductory parts of courses or programs.

The educator should decide (and instruct the case writer, if distinct from the educator) as to what kind of case, within the framework of a specific course, he or she would like before the Case Plan can be constructed. The normal assumption is that for beginners (2,1,1), (1,2,1) or (1,1,2) kinds of cases might be reasonable. It may not make sense to compound the introduction of a difficult concept by adding difficulties in the other two dimensions as well.

The measurements described here are approximate and normative. There is no clear division between a (1,1,1) and a (1,2,1) case in terms of where one ends and the other starts. This must be left to the judgment of the individual educator. In theory, there is a substantial difference between these two. There are, of course, all kinds of cases which could be fractional. However, for the purpose of the original definition, the three divisions per dimension are sufficient.

It is essential for any case writer to position the case along these three dimensions before the Case Plan is written. The Case Difficulty Cube's three-dimensional framework provides the skeleton or the backbone around which the case issue can be built. It may be that lack of information may change a proposed

Concepts, Tools and Process 23

(2,1,3) case to a (2,1,1) case. Occasionally, in subsequent discussions with personnel in the contributing organization, it may become obvious that the original position cannot be kept.

Exhibit 2-2
THE CASE DIFFICULTY CUBE

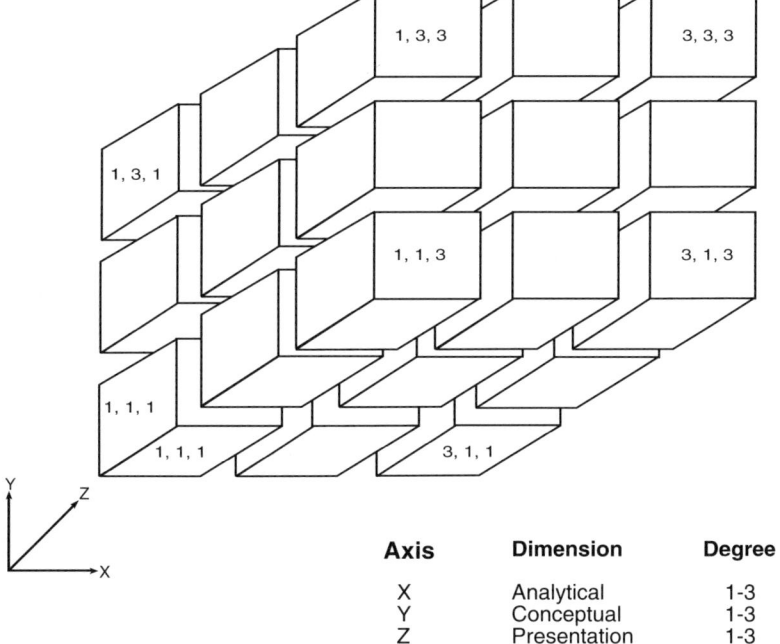

Axis	Dimension	Degree
X	Analytical	1-3
Y	Conceptual	1-3
Z	Presentation	1-3

The case writer is frequently at a loss regarding a supervisor's expectations along the three dimensions of the cube. In the absence of interpretable directions, the case writer focuses on the case issue and second-guesses the framework. Personnel in the contributing organization are equally at a loss in terms of their expectations. A (3,3,3) case is totally different from a (1,1,1) case written about exactly the same issue. An executive may well be disappointed with the end result, expecting a case different from the one actually produced. Therefore, the Case Difficulty Cube is useful as a communication device between supervisor and case writer, and the case writing team and the executives in the contributing organization. The Case Difficulty Cube makes explicit what has too often been implicit.

THE CASE PLAN

The Case Plan constitutes the second major tool for effective case writing. It is the last step of phase one in the three phase case writing process described at the end of this chapter.

The Case Plan has five parts:

1. The opening paragraph.
2. The brief statement of teaching objectives.
3. The proposed organization or outline of the finished case by subtitles.
4. The data requirements list (by subtitles identifying data already available and additional data to be gathered).
5. The time plan.

These five parts will be described in further detail and illustrated through an actual case in Chapter 5.

The Case Plan is useful for the following reasons:

1. It determines the largest percentage of case quality.
2. It establishes the educational objectives for the case.
3. It provides a carefully written communication between case writer and supervisor and between them and the cooperating manager(s), thereby securing a thorough understanding of mutual expectations, roles and tasks.
4. It is short.
5. It helps reduce the total time required to write the case. The time taken to write and modify a Case Plan is but a small fraction of the time needed for a complete case and teaching note.
6. It leads to the provisional release.

Once the case writer and the supervisor agree on the Case Plan, it can be sent to the appropriate person(s) in the contributing organization with an accompanying message. "This is a Case Plan that appeals to us. Is your understanding the same as ours? Are you willing to provide the information we need? And lastly, are you willing to agree to a provisional release? May we come and discuss this with you on this proposed date?"

THE THREE PHASE CASE WRITING PROCESS

The three phase case writing process almost guarantees the final release before significant time and resources have been committed. The recommended process, illustrated in Exhibit 2-3, is summarized below. This chart also indicates the relationship between the time spent on the various activities of the case writing process and the quality of the case. Each activity or step of this process will be elaborated in further chapters.

Phase 1

Case Origin, Lead and Initial Contact

Case origin relates to the decision to write a case for a specific course. Once this decision is made, the case writing process starts with establishing what kind of a case to write and searching for an organization that might supply the case. A phone call, letter or an e-mail to a manager in the organization where the case lead is sought can be used to make the initial contact and set up the first interview.

The first interview permits the case writer to find out whether a potential case exists and whether the organization is willing to supply the data. The general context of this first interview is primarily exploratory. During the first interview, provided a potential case is found, a request is made immediately for a second meeting, ideally within the next few days, to discuss the specific Case Plan(s) forthcoming.

Exhibit 2-3
THE THREE PHASE CASE WRITING PROCESS

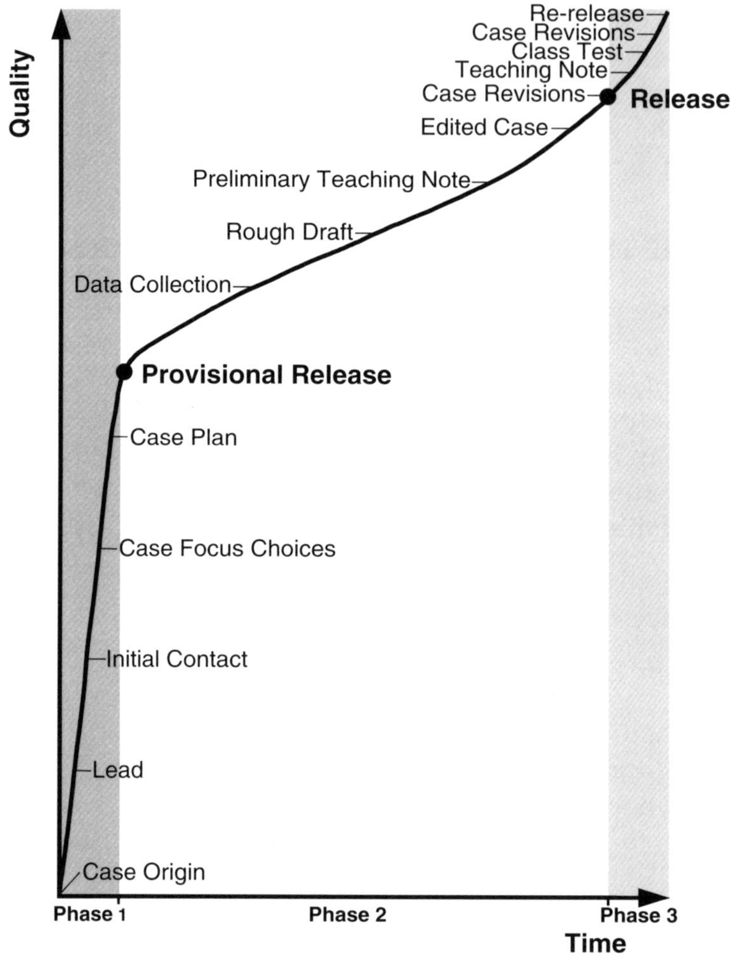

Case Plan Preparation

On the basis of the first interview, one or more Case Plans will be prepared immediately by the case writer and supervisor. Extensive experience with this concept of the Case Plan has shown that it is perfectly reasonable to complete one or more full Case Plans in one day after the initial interview. On the assumption that only one case will be written, the term Case Plan will be used in the subsequent discussion. The case writer and the supervisor discuss the Case Plan, refine it and send it to the contact person in the contributing organization for appraisal.

Second Contact

During the second contact, which may take place in person or on the phone within days of the first interview, the Case Plan will be reviewed with the contact person in the contributing organization. This is the time to discuss any reservations about the correctness of the issue, the availability of the information and the organization's willingness to cooperate.

The selected Case Plan shows the proposed disguise if concern is expressed about the use of the real name(s) of the contributing organization or people working there, or the use of actual figures. The Case Plan also tests the understanding of information given during the first interview.

If agreement to proceed with the case cannot be achieved, it will not be a major problem because little time and effort have been devoted thus far by all parties involved. However, if agreement is reached to proceed with the Case Plan as proposed or modified during the second interview, then the issue of provisional release needs to be raised.

Provisional Release

It is essential that a provisional release be granted as part of the first phase of the case writing process. This provisional release signifies that the contributing organization will make a commitment to cooperate in providing the required information and that, if the final case conforms to the original plan, it will grant the final release. Provisional release is normally verbal but it is wise to confirm it in writing.

Phase 2

Data Collection

The process of gathering the relevant information for the case should be focused, easy and relatively fast, using the data requirements list completed as part of the Case Plan. The manager(s) of the contributing organization will know ahead of time what the case writer needs and will be able to steer her or him to the right sources. Once the missing data have been collected, the case writer can proceed to the rough draft of the case and the preliminary teaching note.

Case Draft and Preliminary Teaching Note

Writing the case draft should be straightforward because the case has already been planned by subtitles, sequence and location of data. This draft is the translation, in sentences and paragraph form, of the data requirements list in the Case Plan.

The purpose of preparing a preliminary teaching note right after the first rough draft of the case is to provide a test for data completeness. Given the preliminary teaching objectives from the Case Plan and the rough draft of the case, the case writer develops a suitable student assignment. The case writer then attempts to answer this assignment on the basis of the information provided in the rough draft. Thus, at a minimum, the preliminary teaching note should contain:

1. a statement of teaching objectives;
2. the suggested student assignment question(s); and
3. the answers to the student assignment.

Developing this preliminary teaching note while the case is still in rough draft form provides an excellent quality control check. It is still easy to collect and include additional information if this is deemed necessary. Once the case has been released, such additional data inclusion becomes much more difficult and may require re-release.

Edited Case

At the editing stage, the emphasis shifts from data completeness, sequence and organization to the standard polishing issues of presentation, grammar, spelling and formatting.

Case Release

During the final release process, the communication back to the contributing organization should basically be, "Here is the case the way we planned it. We would very much appreciate your checking it for accuracy and completeness and we welcome your formal permission to use it." A case written according to plan should meet few, if any, release difficulties.

Sometimes a case is released pending minor revisions. The case writer will make the necessary changes and promptly send the final case to the contact person. All that is left to do is to make the case available for distribution.

Phase 3

Teaching Note Completion, Class Test, Further Case and Teaching Note Revision, and Possible Re-release

While for research assistants the process ends with receiving the final release, the educator using this new case will have to complete additional steps.

The instructor teaching the newly released case will complete the teaching note and the Case Teaching Plan (see Chapter 4 in *Teaching with Cases*) before class.

The first time a case is taught is a major test. It is common to make changes to the case afterwards. Some changes may be editorial in nature, such as a change of wording to avoid ambiguity. Others may address serious gaps and the need for additional information. The case will have to be revised accordingly and may need to go through the release process again if the changes are substantial. Finally, the teaching note will be revised after class to reflect new ideas and concepts that emerged from the class test.

The following chapters will show how each of the steps in the three phase case writing process can be executed quickly and efficiently.

CHAPTER THREE

origin, lead, initial contact

The starting point for writing cases is called case origin. Once the decision has been made to write a case, identifying an organization and an individual willing to co-operate in providing the information for the case is called generating a lead. The first meeting with one or more people in an organization to discuss the possibility of pursuing a case is called the initial contact. This chapter covers case origin, lead and initial contact.

CASE ORIGIN

Our focus on case origin is on the desire to write a new case, as opposed to finding an existing case written by someone else. Case origin results from course planning and recognizing the need to write a case.

The Need to Write a Case

In course planning the essential decisions are selecting the topic areas, deciding where the course starts and ends, and determining how to meet specified educational objectives. Planning courses that use cases is not all that different from planning courses that do not use cases. In our book, *Teaching with Cases*, Chapter 3 addresses this topic. For our purposes here, we focus on why and how an instructor wants to write a new case.

There are existing courses that already include cases and there are existing courses that do not but could. Also, there are new courses that could include cases. Planning new and reviewing existing courses lead to the need to write a case.

Existing Case Courses

When an instructor reviews an existing case course, one reason to write a case is to fill a void or a hole in the course. There is a specific challenge or issue or application not addressed by the cases currently used in the course. For example, in an introductory operations course, a professor might find that none of the current cases raise environmental issues. In an organizational behavior course, the conclusion might be, "I need a case dealing with a human rights issue." In a marketing course, the decision might be, "Having a case on distribution channel selection would be a good addition." Or from a finance course review, a professor might conclude, "I need a case that illustrates the concept of 'Economic Value Added (EVA)'."

A second reason to write a case for an existing case course is to keep the course and the cases used in the course up-to-date. Cases do not last forever. New cases need to be written continuously. New challenges arise in practice; new concepts and techniques are researched and developed; and the economic, political, technological, social and environmental context changes constantly. Writing cases that are chronologically, theoretically and contextually up-to-date is a never-ending challenge. For many experienced case teachers, this constant thinking about existing case courses leads to a continuous search for new cases.

Existing Non-Case Courses or New Course Designs

When an instructor reviews an existing non-case course or designs a new course the question is, "Should cases even be included?" The following justification supports the decision to include cases. The instructor may wish to use a participative approach to learning. Also, the intent of the course may be to combine theory and application. If participants are expected to make a decision or to formulate a judgment based on incomplete or sometimes conflicting information and when alternative solutions exist, cases provide an excellent opportunity for people to learn by doing and by teaching others how and why they arrived at their position. Chapter 1 outlines additional reasons why instructors choose to include cases in course designs.

The Kind of Case to Write

Various factors come into play in deciding what kind of case to write. It is wise to consider not only learning objectives but also student preferences along with other case features.

The Learning Objectives

A logical place to start in determining what kind of case to write is to make a list of all the concepts, theories, tools and techniques covered in the course, plus all the issues and challenges that a student might face in applying the subject matter of the course. Learning objectives relate to the three dimensions of the Case Difficulty Cube as shown in Exhibit 3-1.

If the purpose of writing the new case is to keep the course chronologically and contextually current, then the case writer may conclude, "If I see a case that deals with the current challenges in quality management, I'll write it. If there is one that deals with implementing a balanced scorecard, I'll write that one. If I see a case that deals with a start-up situation, I'll go for it." If the need for writing a case is driven by a particular management decision and its relevant theoretical constructs, then the case writer might say, "I am looking for an example of a break-even analysis involving the pricing of a new product or the viability of a new venture given uncertain demand forecasts or the deletion of a current product or service."

Exhibit 3-1
LEARNING OBJECTIVES AND THE CASE DIFFICULTY CUBE

ANALYTICAL DIMENSION
Difficulty 1 The participant must be able to evaluate a decision taken by others; assess the appropriateness of the decision to the problem or issue identified, whether the appropriate alternatives have been considered and the appropriate decision criteria applied; suggest other alternatives, should the one(s) offered in the case be deemed inadequate; and develop an appropriate action and implementation plan.
Difficulty 2 The participant must be able to assess the issue, decision or opportunity identified on an importance and urgency matrix; assess causes and effects where appropriate; develop alternatives and decision criteria and select the alternative that best fits the quantitative and qualitative assessment of them; develop an action and implementation plan; and specify missing information.
Difficulty 3 The participant must be able to assess the situation and identify problems, issues and challenges. From here the learning objectives are the same as under difficulty 2.
CONCEPTUAL DIMENSION
Difficulty 1 The participant should be able to apply a single, simple theory or concept assigned in readings to a specific case problem or issue without requiring extra explanation of the theory or concept in class.
Difficulty 2 The participant should be able to apply the appropriate theory or concepts or a single complex concept with some assistance or further discussion and explanation in class.

Exhibit 3–1 (continued)

Difficulty 3 The participant should be able to apply a variety of those theories and concepts which might be relevant to the case issues. The participant may require a substantial amount of assistance and explanation in class to understand the integration of these theories or the explanation of the complex theories which are part of the total set.
PRESENTATION DIMENSION
Difficulty 1 The participant should be able to analyze correctly a short, well-organized case, containing no extraneous information, little missing relevant information and presented in a single format.
Difficulty 2 The participant should be able to analyze correctly a medium length case with some disorganization, containing a medium amount of extraneous information, with some missing information and presented in a single or double format.
Difficulty 3 The participant should be able to analyze within a reasonable length of time a long case which may be disorganized, containing lots of extraneous information, a substantial amount of missing information and presented in a variety of formats.

Student Preferences

A second consideration as to the kind of case to write relates to student preferences and interests. Students quickly develop opinions whether cases are good or bad. Given that student motivation and excitement are important components in the overall learning process, paying attention to factors which heighten student interest helps determine what kind of case to write.

Students prefer current cases. Students are also more interested in a case if they can see themselves in the position of the decision maker in the near future or if the issues and challenges are relevant to their career. Likewise, students see the case positively if the organization itself is well-known, respected and not disguised. Cases that are located in a geographical area of the world where the students expect to be working or are currently living are also preferred.

If the issues in the case are urgent and important to the organization, then student reaction tends to be positive. Excitement over the issue also makes a difference. A failure to balance the books by a thousand dollars is not nearly as interesting as a failure to balance the books by several million dollars. Student interest may also quicken with the product or service involved. A case about marketing a new computer game is more exciting than marketing a liver pill. Cases that tell a story, have an interesting dilemma and characters with personalities are also appealing, as are cases that have compelling action requirements. A significant competitive move, an organizational crisis or an urgent request from one's boss motivate participants. On the other hand, cases with solutions already provided tend to demotivate participants.

Short cases tend to be preferred over long cases and well-organized cases over poorly presented ones. A lot of extraneous information is time consuming and annoying. A lot of missing information makes it easy for students to give up. Multiple presentation formats may require too much preparation time. In general, (3, 3, 3) cases tend to be unpopular, unless enough time is allowed for proper preparation before class. At the other extreme, (1, 1, 1) cases can be perceived as trivial.

Therefore, case writers are well advised to consider potential student interest as a major consideration in choosing what kind of case to write.

Other Case Features

Case writers can choose among other case features in deciding the kind of case to write. Case writers select the kind of organization as the setting for the case. For example, should the setting of the company be in manufacturing or in service delivery; should it be a public versus a private company; or a profit versus a not-for-profit organization? There is also a choice involving the particular unit within the organization as well as the level of responsibility of the decision maker. Will the case be set in the head office with the president as the key decision maker or should the case be set in a branch office focussing on a customer service representative? There are also choices around organizational size, functional area, legal structure and geographical setting. Which of these other case features are preferable depend on the course, the learning objectives and student preferences.

The Case Origin Grid

The Case Origin Grid (see Exhibit 3-2) allows a case writer to specify case preferences from a wide variety of possible case features before going to the field. The case features column on the grid is divided into eleven headings that summarize the ideas reviewed above on the need to write a case and the kind of case to write.

Seldom will any educator have a specific requirement across all eleven case features. The course content will be the prime determinant of the case issue or decision and the need for writing the case. Other features may represent opportunities to present a variety of settings and decision makers for cases used in a particular course.

Exhibit 3-2
THE CASE ORIGIN GRID

Course Title: _____ Student Level: _____

CASE FEATURES	CASE PREFERENCES		
	Case #1	Case #2	Case #3… Case #n
1. Course Content			
◆ Theories/Concepts			
◆ Issues/Decisions			
◆ Tools/Techniques			
◆ Other			

Origin, Lead, Initial Contact 39

Exhibit 3-2 (continued)

CASE FEATURES	CASE PREFERENCES		
	Case #1	Case #2	Case #3... Case #n
2. Decision Maker: ■ Responsibility (Board Member, Senior Executive, Owner, Middle Manager, Supervisor, Team Leader, Other) ■ Job Tenure (Experienced, Newly Appointed, Part-time, Contract) ■ Age (Older, Middle-aged, Younger) ■ Gender (Male, Female)			
3. Functional Area: (General Management, Operations, Marketing, Finance, Human Resources, Accounting, Information Systems, Public Administration, International, Other)			
4. Geographical Setting: (Local, Regional, National, International)			
5. Organizational Setting: ■ Manufacturing (Resource, Secondary Industry, Light Industry, Other) ■ Wholesale/Retail (Durable Goods, Consumer Goods, Perishable Goods, Other) ■ Service (Financial, Health Care, Education, Government, Legal, Transportation, Accounting, Consulting, Insurance, Volunteer, Entertainment, Sports, Other)			
6. Product/Service: (Natural Resource, Industrial, Consumer, New, Unique, Other)			

Exhibit 3-2 (continued)

CASE FEATURES	CASE PREFERENCES		
	Case #1	Case #2	Case #3... Case #n
7. **Organization Size:** (Small, Medium, Large)			
8. **Business Unit:** (Head Office, Division, Subsidiary, Joint Venture Partner, Branch, Plant, Office, Department, Cell, Group, Team, Other)			
9. **Ownership:** (Public, Private, Family, Cooperative, Government, Other)			
10. **Legal Structure:** (Limited Company, Partnership, Sole Proprietor, Non-profit, Other)			
11. **Employees:** (Diversity, Union, Other)			

The case preference columns identify where in the course content section cases could or should be used, and any preferences the instructor might have for any of the other ten features. If the instructor has no particular preference, he or she can indicate this by leaving the appropriate space blank.

Exhibit 3-3 illustrates the course content portion of the Case Origin Grid for a professor concluding a review of a first year, MBA required case course in operations management. In this example, the professor has determined a preference for two new cases. The focus in Case #1 is to be on quality and more particularly on deciding whether or not to pursue International Standard Organization (ISO) certification.

Exhibit 3-3
USING THE CASE ORIGIN GRID: A SAMPLE

Course Title: Operations Mgmt. **Student Level:** 1st Yr. MBA

CASE FEATURES	CASE PREFERENCES	
	Case #1	Case #2
1. Course Content		
◆ Theories/Concepts		
Quality	Yes	Yes
Learning Curve		
Materials Requirements Planning		
Push-Pull Systems		
Inventory Models		
Queuing Theory		
Theory of Constraints		
Throughput Time/Cycle Time Capacity		
Continuous Improvement		Yes
Total Quality Management		
Supply Chain Management		
Product Process Matrix		
◆ Issues/Decisions		
ISO Certification	Yes	
Service Delivery		
Competing on Operations Excellence	Yes	
Capacity Expansion		
Manufacturing Strategy		
Technology and Innovation		
◆ Tools/Techniques		
Project Management		
Process Analysis		Yes
Linear Programming		
Gantt Chart		
MTM Tools		
Cause and Effect Diagram		Yes
SMED Analysis		
◆ Other		
Re-engineering		
Trends in Operations	Yes	
Cross-functional Teams		Yes
Robust Design		

For Case #2, the preference is also on quality as related to continuous improvement. The professor would like the case to involve the application of process analysis tools and cause and effect diagrams.

When case writers have identified their case preferences, the search for a lead begins.

CASE LEADS

A person in an organization willing to talk with a case writer about the possible development of a case is called a case lead.

Types of Case Leads

There are two different types of case leads, either company or case writer initiated. Case writers have to be prepared to deal with each kind of lead.

Company or Organization Initiated Lead

This lead is one in which the case writer is invited into an organization by an appropriate contact to write a case that fits the case writer's preferences. For this kind of lead, the task for the case writer is to arrange and prepare for the first interview.

Instructors should encourage their students to provide leads of this kind currently or in the future. "I am always looking for new cases with issues that fit our course. I would be delighted if you would get in touch with me whenever you experience any of the decisions, challenges or issues we have talked about in class."

Case Writer Initiated Lead

This type of lead can be either complete or incomplete. The complete case lead is one in which the case writer knows the appropriate contact in a preferred organization that has the kind of case the case writer is looking for. Here, as well, the case writer has to arrange and prepare for the first interview. A case lead is defined as incomplete whenever a case writer needs to find an organization, an appropriate contact person, or both.

Finding an Appropriate Lead

There are alternative ways of gaining access to contact people in organizations. One is through acquaintances, a second through a cold call, and a third is through an intermediary.

Acquaintances

Case writers can gain access to appropriate leads through their acquaintances and friends. Alumni, past consulting clients and professional association colleagues can be asked, "Can we talk about writing cases in your organization?" "Can you refer me to the best person in your organization to write a case about…..? " "Can you refer me to an appropriate person in another organization that I can talk to about writing cases?"

Experienced case writers actively use colleagues and alumni files to locate "friends" in various organizations and in various parts of the world to gain access to appropriate people. Instructors who teach on executive development programs and who do management consulting have a ready supply of names. For new case writers, the advice is, "Start with your friends first to identify appropriate leads and organizations."

Cold Call

Case writers can also gain access to organizations by making a cold call. A request to write a case via the telephone, e-mail, post-mail or face-to-face to a person unknown to the case writer is called a cold call. Experienced case writers continually have case preferences in mind and are always looking for potential case issues through articles in newspapers, professional journals, trade publications, and in conversations with colleagues and others. When they find such a preferred case, case writers may have to make a cold call. It is appropriate to say, "I saw your name in the newspaper regarding your company's recent expansion decision and I would very much like to talk to you about it."

Intermediary

In gaining access through an intermediary, another person will make the arrangements for the case writer to visit with an appropriate person. That is, the case writer is introduced to a person in an organization through the efforts of a third party. The third party may be known to the case writer or at least known to the case writer's institution. The third party may be inside the intermediary's organization and thus familiar with people and departments. Sometimes the intermediary is outside the target organization but knows a person to contact because of a personal or professional relationship. Intermediary access is often used to gain entry in those countries where personal relationships are extremely important.

For many case writers, finding a case lead can be the first real stumbling block in writing cases. Although they have case preferences, some case writers seem unable or reluctant to take the necessary actions to contact a person in an organization. Excuses are easily offered. "I don't know where to look; I don't know anybody to call, I'll never get people to talk to me; they won't give me access to the information anyway; in our culture, managers will not cooperate in writing cases." Thus far, nowhere in the world have these kinds of excuses proven to be insurmountable.

INITIAL CONTACT

The objective of the initial contact is to determine whether the organization can satisfy the case preferences (see Exhibit 3-2) and whether it is willing to have a case written. Initial contact involves arranging for, preparing for and conducting the first interview. Case writers need to do careful homework to be efficient and effective in these tasks. It is also good practice to find out whether anyone else from the case writer's school or institution is currently writing cases in this organization. In the interest of maintaining positive relationships with the practitioner community, it is a good idea not to wear out the institution's welcome by inundating the organization with case writers. Moreover, it is helpful to find out if cases have been previously written about the organization. If so, at least some company personnel are familiar with the case writing process and the precedent of cooperation in case writing has already been set.

Arranging the Initial Appointment

The case writer makes an appointment before visiting an organization that could become a case contributor. For a case writer/supervisor team, it is normally the instructor who makes the initial appointment. Both the instructor and the case writer meet with the contact person at the arranged time to talk about writing a case. The research assistant's credibility is enhanced considerably by the instructor's presence and support at the initial contact stage.

One of the first questions to answer in making the arrangements for the initial appointment is, "Who is the best person to talk with?" Sometimes the person who provided the lead is not the right person to meet initially. There are two issues concerning the best person to contact initially. First, there is the permission issue, "Who in this organization will permit any case to be written?" Second, there is the specific case issue, "Does the case I prefer exist in this organization?" Sometimes, but not always, the same contact person is in a position to answer both of these questions.

Thus, the best person to meet with for an initial interview is the person in the organization who is most likely to grant release – that is, to give permission to use the case for educational purposes when the case is completed. This person is often the senior person in the organization, in a division, in a particular department or in a unit who is most closely associated with the case writer's area of interest. This individual will normally have the authority to release the case and is most likely to know the situation. It is probable this person will also be able to provide the necessary access to other people in the organization for more particular data the case may require. If the case contact is made by a cold call or through an intermediary, the case writer should make sure that the appointment is made with a senior person in the organization, to avoid surprises and non-release of the case at the end of the process.

A word of caution is in order at this point. Case writers should avoid starting with the legal area, unless a legal case is the desired outcome. Involving the legal department at almost any stage in the case writing process often leads to hassles. Legal departments have a reputation for creating obstacles regarding the release of documents whether disguised or not. When the legal department gets involved, it is often a sign that a case will not be released.

The initial appointment is generally face-to-face, lasts an hour to an hour-and-a-half and almost always takes place at the contact's place of business. The important message to convey in arranging for the initial appointment is that the contact person need only provide his or her time and be willing to talk. The case writer does the work in preparing for and conducting the interview, recognizing that the contact person will want to know why the case writer has come and what the case writing process is all about.

Preparing for the First Interview

While arranging for the initial contact or at the start of the first interview, a case writer needs to be prepared to talk to the contact person about cases, case writing, who does what, why, when and how. Contact persons not familiar with case writing will want to know the answers to these questions before agreeing to proceed.

Cases and the Case Method

The contact person will want to know what a case is and why cases are used. The case writer should be prepared to explain that a case is a description of a decision, challenge or opportunity faced by a person or persons in an organization. A case contains relevant data about the specific situation available to the key person in the case, plus background information about the organization.

Furthermore, the case writer must explain that cases require students to step figuratively into the shoes of the focal person in the case and to make a decision. Students learn about the decision making process through analyzing the information, developing alternatives, making decisions, and formulating an action and implementation plan. They are then asked, in a classroom setting, to communicate and defend their viewpoints before their peers. Cases are also used to test the understanding of theory, to connect theory to application and to develop theoretical insights. Cases enable students to learn by doing and by teaching each other.

The case writer can conclude by saying that the help of practitioners in organizations is essential because a continuing stream of new cases is necessary to stay abreast of current developments in the field.

Roles of the Contact Person and the Case Writer

The contact person will also want to know what he or she is supposed to do and what the case writer does during the case writing process. In response, the case writer can say that the key role for the contact person is to provide information and access to other people in the organization for additional data, to check the case for accuracy and completeness, and provide assistance in its release.

The role of the case writer, on the other hand, is to be a collector and reporter of the facts and the opinions inside the organization. The case writer's task is to get the "story line" straight and to provide sufficient data to allow a case reader to understand the key decision maker's issue(s). The case writer asks questions, collects data and writes the descriptive account. The role of the case writer is not to be a consultant, an evaluator or a judge of decision making effectiveness in the organization.

Confidentiality

At the initial contact stage it is essential to stress the confidential nature of all data throughout the case writing process, until the case is released. This promise allows the contact person to provide information he or she might not normally be willing to share.

Throughout the entire case writing process, case writers maintain strict confidentiality with regard to all information provided by the organization. If preferred, anonymity of the organization, individuals, and some data can be assured through disguise. The final case will be submitted to the organization to verify the accuracy of the data and to indicate its willingness to make it public. A designated person in the organization will be expected to sign a release form permitting the case to be used for educational purposes.

Reasons for Cooperating

Often contacts will want to know why they and their organization should participate in developing a case. The case writer should indicate the first reason is altruistic; it is a donation to the continuing improvement in management education. There are other practical reasons to cooperate. An organization can increase its exposure to future generations of graduates by its contribution to the learning experience of hundreds or even thousands of potential managers. Students may be more likely to identify and seek recruitment with this organization following graduation. Furthermore, the case can be used for internal training, thus forming an effective addition to the learning materials inventory within the organization. Also, people in the organization can benefit from articulating the answers to the questions asked by the case writer. These questions can reinforce the importance of the individuals involved and their respective roles and tasks. Generally, employees react favorably to involvement in the case writing process.

We have used, with great success, a brochure (see Appendix 1) to describe in a concise and clear manner the roles and responsibilities of both practitioners and case writers. It also contains time estimates for the various steps in the case writing process. The intent is to indicate that the case writer does most of the work while the contact person acts primarily as a resource. Our regular practice is to give a copy of this brochure to the contact person and discuss it right at the beginning of the first interview.

Industry/Organization/Contact Person Background Preparation

Once the interview arrangements have been made, case writers should gather information about the organization and the industry before the actual interview. Annual reports, texts, newspaper and magazine articles, web-sites and conversations with colleagues, alumni and friends in the organization are good sources of information. In addition, it is helpful if the case writer can gather background information about the contact person. Obtaining this background knowledge adds to the case writer's confidence and shows the contact person that the case writer is prepared and credible.

Supporting Materials

To enhance the first interview, the case writer should assemble the following items. If it is not possible to forward these in advance, they can be brought to the first interview.

1. **Business Card.** A business card helps the case writer prompt an exchange with the contact person. Exchanging business cards facilitates subsequent communication and ensures that the case writer will know the contact's correct name, address, phone, fax and e-mail information.

2. **Description of the Case Writing Process.** A description of the case writing process including the roles, responsibilities, purposes and steps is very helpful to get the contact person favorably inclined to provide a case (see Appendix 1).

3. **Sample Case.** A sample case allows the contact person to get an idea of what a completed case looks like. Appendix 2 is an example of a short case.

4. **Course Outline.** A course outline allows the contact person to get an idea of the course content, the kinds of materials used and the target student group.

5. **Brochure**. A brochure describing the institution's programs can add to the contact person's understanding.

The Case Shopping List

The Case Shopping List (see Exhibit 3-4) is a vital aid to case writers in telling the contact person what they are looking for as well as in determining whether a preferred case exists in the organization. The Case Shopping List is a set of questions derived from the case preferences identified in the Case Origin Grid. The case preferences are now recast in the context of the specific organization and contact person involved.

The skill in developing the Case Shopping List is to frame the course content (i.e. the theories/concepts, issues/decisions, or tools/techniques listed) for each of the preferred cases on the Case Origin Grid in terms of a decision or action question relevant to the contact person. For example, capacity is a concept; asking a person if he or she recently considered buying additional equipment (to increase capacity) is a question. Motivation is a concept; asking a person if he or she has recently decided or is currently deciding to fire a person (who lacks motivation) is a question. Break-even analysis is a technique; asking a person if he or she has recently raised or is currently considering whether to raise the price of a product (to exceed the break-even point) is a decision. Exhibit 3-4 provides a Case Shopping List of possible questions for the case preferences that the professor identified for the operations course in Exhibit 3-3.

Exhibit 3-4
POSSIBLE CASE SHOPPING LIST QUESTIONS FOR SPECIFIC CASE PREFERENCES

Case Prefer.	Course Content	Case Shopping List Questions
Case #1	Quality ISO 9001 Certification Competing on Operations Excellence Trends in Operations	Have you recently decided or are you currently considering…. 1. applying for ISO 9001 certification? 2. the responses to a major customer request that you become ISO 9001 certified? 3. hiring a consulting firm to help acquire ISO 9001 certification? 4. the size of the budget you need to acquire ISO 9001 certification? 5. confronting a manager who believes you should not seek ISO 9001 certification?
Case #2	Quality Continuous Improvement Process Analysis Cause and Effect Diagram Cross Functional Teams	Have you recently decided or are you currently considering… 1. using a team on a quality initiative? 2. analyzing a process for non-value-adding activities or to improve throughput time? 3. using quality improvement tools, like a cause and effect diagram or a weighted multi-voting technique? 4. making any changes to your processes? 5. changing the size of the reward given to employees for process improvement suggestions?

For a company initiated case lead, the case writer in the first interview can ask the contact person, "Will you please tell me the story about who made the decision, when, why and how?" Even with this kind of lead, it is a good idea to develop a Case Shopping List for several additional case preferences, because the expected case issue may not be available.

Having prepared properly, the case writer is ready to conduct the first interview.

The First Interview

The objective of the first interview is to obtain permission to write a case in the contributing organization and to find at least one affirmative answer to a question on the Case Shopping List.

The first interview guidelines (see Exhibit 3-5) help the case writer achieve the interview objective by providing an agenda. By using these guidelines during the interview, the case writer can mentally or literally check off each item as it is covered.

Beginning the Interview

The first interview typically starts with greetings, introductions and an exchange of business cards. This first part of the interview gives the case writer the opportunity to explain what a case is and why it is used, case writing and what he or she wants from the contact person, including the company's cooperation. The beginning sets the tone for the rest of the interview; and the better the case writer's preparation, the more successful the interview will be.

Conducting the Interview

In conducting the main part of the interview, the case writer starts with the preferred case and the questions on the Case Shopping List. The case writer literally asks the questions, "Have you recently decided to…?" "Have you recently faced a decision where you…?" "Have you recently been asked to…?" "Have

Exhibit 3-5
FIRST INTERVIEW GUIDELINES

1. **Beginning**
    - Thank contact person for agreeing to meet.
    - Exchange business cards.
    - Explain who you are, why you are there, what you would like.
    - Discuss confidentiality and disguise.
    - Ask if company is willing to cooperate.

2. **Conducting**

    Ask the questions on your Case Shopping List for each case preference, "Have you recently decided or are you currently considering..."

    If the contact person says, "No, I haven't considered that," then go to the next question.

    If the contact person says, "Yes, I have made this kind of decision," then ask the person to tell you the "story."
    - What was the decision?
    - How much time was available to make the decision?
    - Who was the decision maker?
    - Why did the decision arise?
    - What was considered?
    - When and where did the decision take place?
    - What alternatives were considered?
    - What happened?

    If the contact person says no to all the Case Shopping List questions for each case preference, then ask one or both of the following questions:
    - What is the most interesting "decision" you faced in the last 12 months? Please tell me the "story."
    - What are your current challenges? Please tell me the "story."

    Allow one to one-and-a-half hours.

3. **Ending**

    Thank the contact person.

    Arrange for a follow-up visit to review the Case Plan(s).

4. **Following**

    As soon as possible, complete the summary notes for each potential case, using the format in Exhibit 3-6.

you recently been involved with…?" If the contact person says, "No," then the case writer moves to the next question for the preferred case. The case writer proceeds down all the case preferences and the related questions until at some point the contact person says, "Well, yes I have done…," or "I decided to…," or "I just started using…" When the "Yes" response occurs, the case writer seizes the opportunity to ask, "Please tell me the story of how, who, when, where and why you did it."

Case writers must exercise gentle control to keep the interview on track. The danger lies in the contact person's tendency to describe the history of the organization, the kinds of processes and procedures used, and the products and services delivered, instead of identifying key decisions. Therefore, the case writer needs to keep the contact person focused on the relevant Case Shopping List question. The case writer, recognizing that he or she will soon need to develop a Case Plan for the case, needs to clearly understand what the decision was; who was involved; what triggered the decision to be taken or the recommendation to be made in the first place; when it happened; what key aspects and alternatives were considered; and what the major outcomes were. It may be possible to talk about two or three case preferences within the hour or so of the first interview.

As each potential case is discussed, the case writer is continually reflecting on the case preferences, "Is there a case here that I want? Does this decision fit my purposes?" Some great issues may arise that do not fit the case writer's needs. For example, the decision was made too long ago, and by the time the case appears in the classroom it will be dated. Or, the issue might make a good finance case but the case writer wants one in the marketing area. In these instances, the case writer should be prepared to move the interview on to another case preference.

Sometimes in the first interview, the case writer asks all of the Case Shopping List questions for each case preference and each time the contact person says, "No, I haven't faced that. No, I don't use that in our organization. No. No. No." All is not lost because there are two further questions that a case writer can always ask. One question is, "What is the most interesting decision you faced during the last 12 months?" A second question is, "What decisions are you currently working on?" The answers here may have greater interest for the contact person, and fleshing out the story-line details can often produce a great case. Very rarely should a case writer walk away from the first interview empty-handed unless, of course, the contact person has indicated a preference not to proceed. Even if there is an apparent fit with a Case Shopping List question, the open-ended questions above may reveal an even better case.

Ending the Interview

Ending the first interview by the agreed-upon time is important, unless the contact person is completely free and wants to keep talking. Case writers should not overstay their welcome during the initial contact. Before ending the interview, however, it is important for the case writer to establish the next steps and to arrange for the next meeting. A typical ending is, "Thank you very much for your time and for the information. I enjoyed listening to your experiences and I look forward to meeting with you again next Tuesday. In the meantime, I'll send you a plan of a possible case that I would like to pursue in your organization. We can talk about this plan on Tuesday. Thank you very much. See you next week."

Following the Interview

Very shortly after the interview, it is good practice to review one's interview notes for completeness, possibly in the reception area or parking lot of the contributing organization. Time is of the essence while the details are still fresh. Exhibit 3-6, the potential case summary form, helps to organize the key facts from the interview. Following the first interview, the case writer makes case focus choices and resolves the issue of disguise if necessary.

Exhibit 3-6
POTENTIAL CASE SUMMARY NOTES

Potential Case # _____
What was the issue/decision/challenge/action?
Who was the decision maker or focal person (name and position)?
Why did it happen (i.e. action triggers)?
When and where did the decision take place?
Time available to make decision or recommendation:
What was considered (quantitative, qualitative)?
Alternatives reviewed (if any):
What happened (if available)?

CHAPTER FOUR

case focus choices and disguise

After the initial visit to the contributing organization and before developing the Case Plan, the case writer is faced with key choices regarding 1) issue, 2) timing including action triggers and 3) decision maker. The case writer determines the largest part of the case quality by these three choices. Disguise is the last topic discussed in this chapter.

CASE FOCUS CHOICES

1. The Choice of Issue

The choice of issue, decision, problem or opportunity for the case relates closely to the Case Shopping List discussed in Chapter 3. If more than one issue is available in the contributing organization, the preferred case option may be selected on the basis of best fit with the Case Origin Grid, also covered in Chapter 3. A specific case issue may also be chosen because people in the contributing organization are excited about it, the issue may be more recent or the information will be easier to collect.

2. The Choice of Timing

The choice of issue and its timing are closely interrelated. Two major timing choices are made during issue selection: the story line cut and the decision frame cut.

The Story Line Cut

Every issue has a chronology or story line. Some events happen at the same time, before or after others and each story contains major decision points. The case writer has to understand the story. What happened when, where and why? At what stages were major decisions made by whom and why? What were the consequences? Once the case writer is clear regarding the answers to these questions, he or she can make the choice as to where to cut the story. Exhibit 4-1 illustrates potential story line cuts a case writer could consider.

Exhibit 4-1
POTENTIAL STORY LINE CUTS

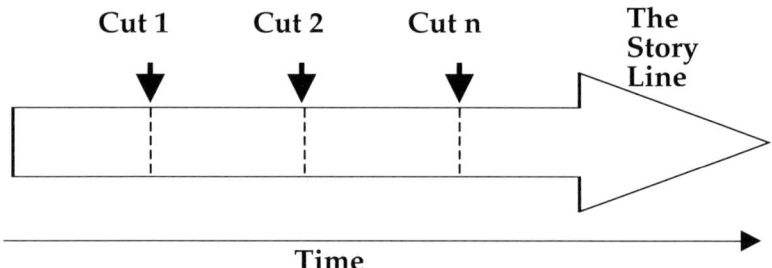

An example of a story line was extracted from the notes written by a participant at one of our Brazilian case writing workshops immediately after the initial interview.

During the interview the case writer learned the company had not achieved sales targets for a recently introduced product. The situation was sufficiently serious to call in a consultant to ask for advice. This consultant then analyzed the situation and came to the conclusion that sales management within the company was the prime cause for the sales problem. Subsequently, the consultant recommended that the incumbent sales manager be replaced by a candidate preferred by the consultant. After interviewing this candidate, management agreed the qualifications of this individual appeared satisfactory. Next, a new problem emerged. How to dismiss the current sales manager who still had an employment contract with the company?

It is possible to create a table identifying this sequence of potential story line cuts with the corresponding dates and potential decision maker. Exhibit 4-2 is based on the case writer's data collected during the initial interview covering a period starting in August and lasting almost a year. Question marks behind dates and decision makers indicate the case writer was not sure. The interview notes reveal at least nine potential story line cuts.

It is the case writer's responsibility to select the story line cut that best fits the educational objectives of the course. For a marketing course a story line cut at points 1 or 5 might be more interesting, for a legal course a story line cut at number 9, for a general management course a cut at numbers 2, 3,4 or 8, and for a consulting course a cut at 2, 3, 4, 5, 6 or 7.

The potential story line cuts identified by a case writer obviously have course usefulness implications well beyond the specific course or program for which the case writer is trying to find the case. It is possible to pass such potential case options to others who are also looking for new cases. Occasionally, a series of cases can be written about the same story line in one organization for one course or covering a variety of courses. Such a case series has excellent integrative potential.

Exhibit 4-2
POTENTIAL STORY LINE CUTS FOR
THE BRAZILIAN CASE EXAMPLE

Potential Story Line Cut	Issue Focus	Timing	Decision Maker
1	problem identification	*August 4 - January 3*	Marketing or Sales Manager
2	hiring a consultant	*January 3- February 5*	President or Marketing Manager
3	consultant terms of reference	*Early March ?*	President or Marketing Manager
4	consultant selection	*Late March ?*	President or Marketing Manager
5	problem analysis and definition	*April ?*	Consultant
6	consultant presentation	*May ?*	Consultant
7	evaluation of potential sales manager candidates	*June 11-17*	Consultant
8	employee selection	*later in June*	President or Human Resources Manager
9	employee dismissal	*July 3*	President or Human Resources Manager or Legal Counsel

The Decision Frame Cut

Once the story line cut has been decided, the next timing decision involves the decision frame cut. Every decision in any organization when viewed from a case writing perspective has six standard decision frame cuts starting from 1) when the need for a decision has not even been identified, through 2) issue awareness and information gathering, 3) analysis and alternative generation, 4) decision, 5) implementation to 6) evaluation. These six decision frame cut options are shown in Exhibit 4-3.

Whereas the story line changes with every case, the decision frame cut always offers the same six options.

Exhibit 4-3
THE SIX DECISION FRAME CUT OPTIONS

```
           6                      1
       Evaluation           Issue Not
                            Identified

   5                                  2
Implementation                     Awareness
                                      and
                                  Information
                                   Gathering

           4                      3
        Decision            Analysis and
                             Alternative
                              Generation
```

Combining Story Line and Decision Frame Cuts

Exhibit 4-4 combines the story line cut options as shown in Exhibit 4-1 and the decision frame cut options are shown in Exhibit 4-3. The diagram in Exhibit 4-4 is a crucial one for every case writer to consider when trying to decide on the issue and timing for a potential case. An understanding of the options provided in any story line and the accompanying decision frames allows the case writer to make an informed choice.

The story line and decision frame cuts chosen by the case writer cannot be beyond the actual situation in the organization, but can cover earlier story line and decision frame cut options. Thus, in the Brazilian example, if at the time of the case writer's visit no decision has yet been taken regarding the current sales manager's potential dismissal, this decision becomes the latest story line cut. The decision frame cut option can be placed prior to this decision, but not after it.

**Exhibit 4-4
THE COMBINED STORY LINE
AND DECISION FRAME CUTS**

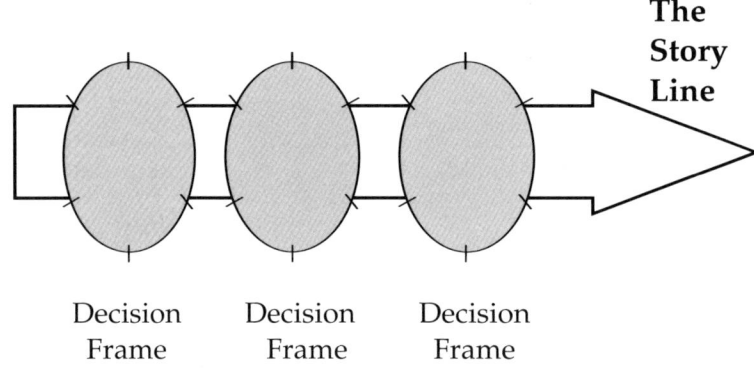

Decision   Decision   Decision
Frame   Frame   Frame

In the example of the Brazilian company, story line Cut 1 in Exhibit 4-2 was the preferred choice of the case writer. The time period was from August to January. After the introduction of a major new product line, launched in the beginning of August, sales volumes were not meeting expectations. Where in the August to January decision frame does it make sense to cut this case? Is it in August as the first orders come in below expectations? Is it in October or November when reorders do not appear? The decision frame cut option table shown in Exhibit 4-5 outlines these two options. Also included are a few suggestions for potential "action triggers."

Exhibit 4-5
THE DECISION FRAME CUT OPTION TABLE FOR STORY LINE CUT 1 OF BRAZILIAN CASE EXAMPLE

Decision Frame Cut	Decision Phase	Decision Point and Date	Potential Action Trigger	Potential Maker Decision
1	Issue not identified	Product launch Early August	First market reaction	President, Marketing Manager or Product Manager
2	Awareness and information gathering	Sales reports Sept.-Nov.	First sales reports or a major customer does not reorder	President, Marketing Manager or Product Manager

It is good practice to create a potential story line cut option table as done in Exhibit 4-2 and decision frame cut option table as done in Exhibit 4-5 to help select the best case.

Action Triggers

Action triggers are those events or incidents within an organization that cause one or more persons to respond. These are the "wake-up" calls, the "attention getters" or the reasons why a person in an organization becomes concerned with an issue. Typical action triggers are listed in Exhibit 4-6.

Action triggers are at the core of the timing options available to the case writer. The action trigger and its associated real life timing make the case believable for the case reader. Consider the following two examples:

A. For the last ten years, Joan Winters, President of Western Electronics, a control system producer located in Manchester,

England, had been dissatisfied with the performance of her executive assistant. In December ..._{year}..., she was thinking of firing him.

B. On December 7, ..._{year}..., at 3:30 p.m., Joan Winters, President of Western Electronics, a control system producer located in Manchester, England, received a telephone call from the purchasing manager of the firm's largest client: "Joan, why did your firm not bid on the Sussex job?" Joan suddenly realized that her firm's bid on this very large job had missed a deadline because her assistant had failed to send it out in time.

Version A is obviously not believable because its action trigger is not identified.

Exhibit 4-6
TYPICAL ACTION TRIGGERS

A communication. A meeting with or telephone call, memo, report, fax, e-mail or letter from a customer, boss, fellow employee, supplier, task force member(s), union or government official, journalist, activist, shareholder, or concerned citizen requesting or demanding a response.
A major internal event. A major event such as a serious equipment failure, a fire, a corporate financial collapse, a merger or takeover, a death or prolonged sickness, an electrical power outage, the loss or gain of a significant customer, the departure or entry of a key person, a major opportunity identified, a significant competitive action, results not meeting expectations or planned targets.
A major external event. A major technological, political, social, economic or environmental change, a new government law or regulation, a major competitive action.

The preciseness of the timing becomes an indicator of the urgency of the issue. With what time specificity should the action trigger in the case be reported? Should it be the year, the month, the week, the day, the hour or the minute? Very seldom should it be the year only, because the timing is then too vague. The action trigger starts the clock ticking for the focal person in the case. Somewhere in the case, often in the concluding paragraph, the case writer will state the deadline for action. And the time between the action trigger and the deadline is the period for the focal person in the case to gather information, analyze it, develop decision criteria and alternatives, and to decide on the best action/implementation plan or to evaluate past actions and decisions. The urgency of the issue, decision or problem in the case is determined by the length of time between the action trigger and the deadline. There is a huge difference between a situation in which the key decision maker is given one hour to resolve an issue versus a situation in which three months are available.

Too many case writers have difficulty identifying the correct actual action triggers in cases. Therefore, they start their cases with eloquent phrases like:

> In August ...$_{year}$..., Roberta Angelina was gazing out of her office window at the graceful swans floating on the lake in front of the company's head office trying to think of a better way of promoting the new line of health foods the company was planning to introduce.

Compare this version to the following:

> At 2:30 p.m. on August 13, ...$_{year}$..., Roberta Angelina, marketing associate at Health Foods Inc., had a meeting with the vice president, Joan Alders. Joan said, "I don't like the promotion plan you prepared for our new product line. I'll give you two weeks to come up with a better one."

Some case writers seem to believe that it is their visit with the focal person in the case that triggers this person into dreaming up cases on the spot. This is nonsense. The case writer's job is to get the relevant and exact details of the story line and the decision frame. What were the action triggers? Dates, times, places and individuals involved in the actual story line and decision frame are key components of action triggers so that the reader of the case can understand why action is important and what the time remaining for action is.

3. The Choice of Decision Maker or Focal Person

The third key choice early in the Case Plan concerns the decision maker. Often, this choice is simple, it is the person interviewed. Sometimes, as in the Brazilian case example, it may be possible to address the issue from various management perspectives. The Brazilian story could be presented from the position of the president, marketing manager or consultant to name just a few. The story line cut table in Exhibit 4-2 and the decision frame cut table in Exhibit 4-5 have already identified various options regarding focal persons in the case. The choice of decision maker in case writing depends on the case writer, the case preferences as identified on the Case Origin Grid and the willingness of the focal person to cooperate in the case writing process. Most cases identify a single person as the focal person.

Once the three key choices regarding issues, timing and decision maker have been resolved along with the appropriate action trigger, the case writer needs to decide what disguise is required, if any.

DISGUISE

Disguise is used to obtain the release of a case or case data which might not be released otherwise. Disguise is, therefore, needed to preserve the anonymity of the source and the security of the data. The educator's concern with disguise is different from the manager's whose organization supplies the case information. The educator would like to obtain a useful educational vehicle and prefers realism and full believability. The manager, on the other hand, may only be concerned that his or her organization not be identifiable or that sensitive information not be traceable or reproduced in its original form. These objectives are often directly opposed to one another.

Sometimes there are good educational reasons for disguise even if the contributing organization is willing to release an undisguised version. For example, students may wish to telephone or e-mail the manager to ask what really happened. Sometimes, also, there may be a need to protect the contributing organization from dangers the manager does not recognize. For example, confidential information could fall into the hands of a competitor or the manager fails to perceive that readers might view his or her actions as inappropriate.

Disguise of Information

There are many ways in which a case may be disguised. The most important decision involves the use of the actual name of the contributing organization. Changing the name requires little case writing effort, but destroys the strongest student identification asset. For organizations which are small or relatively unknown, this issue is different from those which are well-known. The well-known organization is likely to attract the students' interest, and the educator will often try to preserve the name. Even if the name of the organization is not changed, names of personnel often are. For the case writer, personal name changes are normally not an issue, but may well be perceived as crucial by people in the organization. Dates and locations may be altered also. Numerical data, like sales figures, costs, etc., may be changed by multiplying all figures by a constant like .93 or 1.1 or presenting them as percentages. An attempt to disguise numerical data by multiplying with an unusually large constant may conflict with other information. For example, the work force is too small or large in relation to the sales volume. The profit on a product or service line does not agree with the income statement. With numerical data it is the relationship between the numbers and not the actual figure that is important. The organization's product or service may be changed to a similar one or a totally different one. The industry may be changed as well.

The Disguise of the Organization's Name

In disguising organizational names it is not possible to call the disguised company by the name of another real company. It is wrong to rename the company by a competitor's name, for example, Ford into General Motors. It is advisable to check a registry of company names to assure no identically named company exists. Using letters like Company X takes too much away from the real case. Students know "Company X" does not really exist and hence using letters or numbers for company names is not a popular case writing practice.

If the name of a company is disguised, the names of individuals need to be disguised also.

The Disguise of Individual Names

If names of individuals in the case need to be disguised, it is wise to avoid the same initial letters and to preserve the sex and national or cultural identity to the maximum extent possible. Thus, for a case written in Hong Kong, changing a Mr. Wong to Ms. Williamson sends an incorrect message on all three counts.

Occasionally, case writers try to be humorous and use names like Mr. Computer for the MIS manager and Ms. Greenshades for an accountant. Such phony disguise attempts prevent students from taking the case seriously.

Some people have suggested that every person in the case should be referred to in a gender neutral style, like Person A or Person 3. The drawbacks here are obvious and such neutrality has not become a case writing practice.

The Disguise of Other Information

All changes for disguise purposes require great care to preserve the believability of the issue. A major location change may, for example, impact labor rates, local, state or provincial regulations, taxes, climatic considerations and market conditions. Product or service industry changes are often most difficult to accomplish without harming, in at least some way, the reality of the original situation. The simpler the case, the easier disguise often becomes. An introductory investment proposal case, focusing on the calculation of future cash flows, falls into a totally different category from a broad strategy case. Therefore, differences of opinion exist among educators about disguise strategies. Someone writing simple direct cases may be less concerned, and agree more quickly to disguise, than someone writing complex cases.

There seems to be a trend away from full disguise and towards greater use of the contributing organization's name. Whether educators are becoming bolder in their demands or managers less fearful about disclosure is difficult to determine. Disclosure is more likely when managers are familiar with the case method and the purpose of the case.

The further the case writer goes in disguising information from names to numbers to products to industries, the more the case issue becomes fictionalized and hence not a reflection of a particular decision maker's reality. It is important not to change a real case into a fictional one by excessive disguise. Therefore, the minimum of disguise necessary to obtain release should be sought.

Disguise Approach

Seasoned case writers develop a standard approach with respect to disguise for use with managers.

It is best that the case writer clarifies whether a disguise is required and what kind during the initial interview. If a disguise will be required, it is sound practice to show the disguise chosen directly in the case title and the opening paragraph. This way, the focal person in the case can immediately see that this sensitive area has been addressed satisfactorily, building confidence that other promises by the case writer will also be kept.

Once the case focus choices regarding issue, timing and decision maker have been resolved and the disguise requirements have been met, the case writer can proceed with the Case Plan.

CHAPTER FIVE

case plan and provisional release

The Case Plan is the key document in completing the first phase of the case writing process. The Case Plan identifies the focus and purpose of the case, its organization, contents and schedule for completion. It is a vital communication tool between the case writer and the focal person in the case as well as between the case writer and supervisor. The major part of this chapter covers the development of the Case Plan followed by a discussion of the provisional release.

THE CASE PLAN

The Case Plan requires the case writer to be specific regarding the case focus choices before the case is actually written. The Case Plan also requires the contributing organization to be specific about disguise, data availability and willingness to grant the provisional release.

The Case Plan has five components:

1. The opening paragraph.
2. The brief statement of teaching objectives.
3. The proposed organization or outline of the case by subtitles.
4. The data requirements list.
5. The time plan.

1. The Opening Paragraph

The opening paragraph will be the first paragraph of the final case. In the case method the reader is asked to put him or herself in the position of the decision maker. "If you were in the position of Manager X, what would you do in this situation?" is a normal case assignment question. The intent of the opening paragraph is to present a capsule of the issue the reader will face. The sooner the reader of the case understands which position in the organization to assume and what task to undertake, the better and faster the reader can proceed with the reading and analysis. In Chapter 3 of *Learning with Cases* the Short Cycle Process focuses on the opening paragraph. And the Case Preparation Chart starts with the standard who, what, where, when, why and how questions, largely based on the opening paragraph.

The opening paragraph can be seen as an eyepiece or a lens that directs the reader of the case through the subsequent information. The intent is that the opening paragraph will clearly indicate what the final case will focus on. The opening paragraph will also be used as the key discussion piece with the contributing organization's contact, and between case writer and supervisor during the initial stages of case writing.

Considerable care will be required to polish the opening paragraph to perfect form. Because it is only one paragraph and should normally contain less than six sentences, it does not take very long to review and rewrite one's own or edit someone else's opening paragraph. Until the opening paragraph is clear, concise and complete, there is no point in working on the other components of the Case Plan.

The Brazilian Case Example

The educator involved in the Brazilian case example (see Chapter 4) wanted to write her own case. She was looking for a case which could be used as an introduction to the four P's in marketing. She intended the case for her course in a parttime degree program involving students who held full-time jobs. With these general objectives in mind, she visited a local company in Curitiba, Brazil, where a number of ideas were discussed with the president during the initial company contact.

Here is her first draft of the opening paragraph.

The _____ Corporation had problems in the marketing area. The management of the Corporation obtained the services of a consultant who identified the main problem in the sales area. The consultant recommended, among other things, that a new marketing manager be hired who would bring new life to the sales area. Management interviewed the consultant's recommended candidate and was favorably impressed. Unfortunately, the Corporation still had a contract with the existing manager which had another two years left.

The Opening Paragraph Checklist

Over the years of instructing thousands of case writers on how to write good cases quickly we have developed the opening paragraph checklist (see Exhibit 5-1). Its 11 questions assist the case writer in ensuring his or her opening paragraph is clear, concise and complete. It is also helpful for others as a means of evaluating the opening paragraph.

Each of these 11 opening paragraph checklist questions will be discussed further followed by the answer to each question as applied to the Brazilian case example.

Question 1. Is the decision maker identified by name and position?

Naming the person holding the position personalizes the case. The reader of the case is expected to assume the position of the decision maker in reading and interpreting case data.

Exhibit 5-1
THE OPENING PARAGRAPH CHECKLIST

1. Is the decision maker identified by name and position?
2. Is the time of the case clear?
3. Is the location of the organization identified?
4. Is the issue, decision, problem or opportunity clearly identified?
5. Is the issue, decision, problem or opportunity sufficiently interesting for use in class?
6. Has the story line cut been made at the right time? Will moving this cut forward or backward result in a better case?
7. Has the decision frame cut been made at the right time? Will moving this cut forward or backward result in a better case?
8. What is the action trigger?
9. What is the expected position of the case on the Case Difficulty Cube?
10. Will the case be disguised and to what extent?

	Disguise Required	
	Yes	No
a) Company name		
b) Names of personnel		
c) Date		
d) Location		
e) Numerical data		
f) Product		
g) Industry		

11. Are the case title and the names chosen for the persons in the case appropriate?

Answer. The decision maker is not identified by name or position.

Question 2. Is the time of the case clear?

The date of the case places the issue, decision, problem or opportunity into a specific time period. Cases are time-bound by the context in which they are set. Readers are expected to understand the economic, cultural, social, political and technological contexts implied by the date. Including these background data would make the case too long.

Answer. The date of the case is not identified. It should be more specific as to day, month and year.

Question 3. Is the location of the organization identified?

The location of the organization along with the date provide the context within which the contributing organization operates. The largest part of every case never gets written. Given the date and the location of the case, the reader is normally expected to provide the background from the generalized knowledge he or she has acquired. Cases do not travel well. Cases need to be written for the various geographical and cultural settings within which students expect to work.

Answer. The location of the organization is not identified.

Question 4. Is the issue, decision, problem or opportunity clearly identified?

The reader needs to know what kind of analytical task is required for what kind of issue, decision, problem or opportunity. This question is tied directly to the analytical dimension of the Case Difficulty Cube.

Answer. It is not clear which of the various issues mentioned in the opening paragraph should be the focus of this case.

Question 5. Is the issue, decision, problem or opportunity sufficiently interesting for use in class?

This question has been addressed in Chapter 3. Whether a case issue is likely to be of interest to case readers is always a worthwhile concern for any case writer.

Answer. Different issues in the Brazilian example could be interesting to students after the focus has been sharpened.

Question 6. Has the story line cut been made at the right time? Will moving this cut forward or backward result in a better case?

It is good practice to envisage different case possibilities by moving the story line cut forward or backward as discussed in Chapter 4. By moving the story line cut the case writer may change the issue, timing and decision maker.

Answer. The first draft of the opening paragraph shows several story line cut possibilities (see Exhibit 4-2). Each story line cut leads to a different opening paragraph. Exhibit 5-2 shows the nine possibilities in opening paragraph form, incorporating additional information the case writer gathered during the initial interview. The choice of opening paragraph depends on the Case Origin Grid (see Chapter 3) and the choice of case focus (see Chapter 4).

Exhibit 5-2
POTENTIAL OPENING PARAGRAPHS FOR THE BRAZILIAN CASE EXAMPLE

Story Line Cut 1. On December 7, ...$_{year}$..., Sr. Da Silva, Marketing Manager at Delbar, a Brazilian industrial products producer located in Curitiba, Brazil, received the four-month sales report for Milo, a new product launched in August. Sales were much lower than forecast and Sr. Da Silva wanted to determine why.

Story Line Cut 2. On January 3, ...$_{year}$..., Sr. Perreira, President of Delbar, a Brazilian company, had just finished a meeting with Sr.

Case Plan and Provisional Release 77

Exhibit 5-2 (continued)

Da Silva, the Marketing Manager, to discuss Milo, a recently introduced new product. Milo had failed to live up to its sales expectations and Sr. Perreira was concerned that Sr. Da Silva could not explain why Milo sales were so low.

Story Line Cut 3. On March 3, ...$_{year}$..., Sr. Perreira, President of Delbar, a Brazilian company, was trying to decide what the scope should be for a consulting study and how much he was willing to pay for consulting advice. The recent market failure of Milo, a new product, was the primary reason for bringing in a consultant, but should this be the consultant's sole focus?

Story Line Cut 4. On March 3, ...$_{year}$..., Sr. Perreira, President of Delbar, a Brazilian company, was reviewing three proposals from marketing consultants. A recently introduced product, Milo, had failed. Sr. Perreira wondered which consultant could give the best advice for corrective action.

Story Line Cut 5. It was late April ...$_{year}$..., and Sra. Polzin, a marketing consultant in Curitiba, Brazil, was analyzing the information she had collected regarding a new product introduction failure. She knew the client's president was anxious to receive her views quickly, but she wanted to be sure her analysis was sound.

Story Line Cut 6. In mid-May ...$_{year}$..., Sra. Polzin, a marketing consultant in Curitiba, Brazil, had completed her analysis of a failed new product introduction and was ready to plan her presentation to the president of the client company.

Story Line Cut 7. In early June ...$_{year}$..., Sra. Polzin, a marketing consultant in Curitiba, Brazil, was reviewing potential candidates for the marketing manager position at Delbar, one of her clients. She had four potential candidates in mind and had to rank each one.

Story Line Cut 8. It was June 22, ...$_{year}$..., and Sr. Perreira, President of Delbar, a Brazilian company, had just interviewed Sr. Gomez, a potential candidate for the position of marketing manager recommended by a consultant. As he reviewed the resume and the interview, he was trying to determine if this was the right person for the job.

Exhibit 5-2 (continued)

Story Line Cut 9. On July 4, ...$_{year}$..., Sr. Garcia, Personnel Manager of Delbar, a Brazilian company, had a meeting with Sr. Perreira, the President. Sr. Perreira said, "You know we are anxious to bring in a new marketing manager quickly, but we still have an employment contract with Sr. Da Silva. How much will it cost us to get him out of here?"

Question 7. Has the decision frame cut been made at the right time? Will moving it forward or backward result in a better case?"

By changing the decision frame cut, the case writer shifts the analytical task for the student among the six options identified in Exhibit 4-3.

Answer. Two decision frame cut possibilities are discussed in Chapter 4 and two potential opening paragraph versions for these cuts are provided in Exhibit 5-3.

Since the Brazilian case writer wished to focus on the product introduction phase of Milo rather than the consulting and personnel issues, the following two opening paragraphs are set in the August to January period story line cut. These opening paragraph options also contain additional information the Brazilian case writer obtained during the initial company contact.

Question 8. What is the action trigger?

Without an action trigger the case reader is left wondering what initiated the need for action and is unable to determine the importance and urgency of the issue.

Answer. There are many potential action triggers identified in the Brazilian opening paragraph, but the appropriate one depends on the story line and decision frame cut decision.

EXHIBIT 5-3
POTENTIAL OPENING PARAGRAPHS FOR THE TWO DECISION FRAME CUTS

Decision Frame Cut 1. On August 4, ...$_{year}$..., Sr. Da Silva, Marketing Manager at Delbar, a Brazilian producer of industrial products located in Curitiba, Brazil, received a telephone call from the purchasing manager at Brascon, a major customer. "Thanks for the Milo samples you sent, but my maintenance people tell me that this new product of yours is no better than the old one, it's just more expensive."

Decision Frame Cut 2. On November 5, ...$_{year}$..., Sr. Da Silva, Marketing Manager at Delbar, a Brazilian company, received the disappointing three-month sales report for Milo, a recently introduced new product.

Question 9. What is the position of the case on the Case Difficulty Cube?

At the opening paragraph stage, it is useful to position the intended case on the Case Difficulty position.

Answer. For the Brazilian example it is impossible to establish the Case Difficulty Cube position until the issue and timing decisions have been made.

Question 10. Will the case be disguised and to what extent?

Before the opening paragraph is finalized, the disguise chosen, if any, should reflect the wishes of the contributing organization (see Chapter 4). The list provided in Exhibit 5-1 covers the most frequently used disguise options. The greater the number of options exercised, the farther the case departs from reality and the wisdom of pursuing this case may be questioned.

Answer. The Brazilian case writer knew that the name of the organization and the names of the decision makers needed to be disguised.

Question 11. Are the case title and names chosen for the persons in the case appropriate?

The two common choices for case titles are:

1. the name of the organization, real or disguised;
2. the name of the key decision maker in the case, real or disguised and, possibly, the position held in the organization.

Occasionally, the case title may describe the type of issue, decision, problem or opportunity addressed in the case.

Answer. No case title or names of individuals were provided in the opening paragraph. Case titles could be "Delbar," "Milo" or "The Milo Launch." A combination of the above could also be used: "Delbar—The Milo Launch." For the appropriateness of names assigned to organizational personnel, please see the discussion on disguise in Chapter 4.

The Case Title

It is generally not a good idea to identify the case by an unusual or funny or analytical title. Examples for the Brazilian case would be: "Milo's Miseries" or "The Product Launch that Missed the Champagne Bottle" or "Milo's Ill-conceived Entry into the Brazilian Market." It is important, especially with disguised cases, that every case be perceived as a real life situation and nothing in the title should raise doubts about that in the reader's mind. Moreover, cases are often used by different instructors for different purposes and a neutral title allows for such treatment. For example, the Brazilian case was intended to reinforce the four P's of marketing, but it could also be used in a forecasting class or in a project management or new product introduction class.

For series cases or cases written about the same organization on different topics at different times, case titles are often indicated by letters after the organization's name. A good example would be Delbar(A), Delbar (B), Delbar (C).

Additional Observations about Opening Paragraph Writing

The quick sketching of the various case possibilities in opening paragraph form is a useful device to help any case writer determine the best place to focus the final case choice. Should the case writer work for a supervisor or with colleagues who might eventually teach the case, the range of opening paragraph options can be shared and preferences determined before the time consuming part of writing the case begins.

This process of drafting potential opening paragraphs can be started immediately after the initial interview. We have written opening paragraphs in the contributing organization's lobby or parking lot just to make sure that we have captured some key ideas. It is always possible later to expand the range of possibilities, but having a few starting points is certainly helpful.

The writing of opening paragraphs should be a standard skill for all case writers and one easily acquired. It does not take long to write an opening paragraph, read and revise it. The checklist in Exhibit 5-1 is a good guide for standard information to be included. Who, what, when, where and why are not difficult questions to answer.

The Brazilian case opening paragraph examples show how differences in opening paragraphs lead to different cases. A photographer can walk into a room and come out with totally different photos, depending on what he or she chose to focus on: the furniture, the view out of the window or a person in the room. It is exactly the same with case writing.

A significant amount of creativity in case writing is spent in developing the opening paragraph. That is why in our workshops we spend a lot of time on the creation and polishing of opening paragraphs. Getting the opening paragraph right facilitates every subsequent step in the case writing process. Once the three key decisions regarding issue, timing and decision maker have been fixed, the rest of the case development process becomes largely technical.

The final opening paragraph selected by the case writer for the Brazilian example was:

DELBAR

On November 5, 2000, Sr. Da Silva, Marketing Manager at Delbar, a Brazilian producer of industrial products, located in Curitiba, Brazil, reviewed the three-month sales report for Milo, a recently introduced new product. Sr. Da Silva was disappointed that forecasts were not met and wanted to determine what, if anything, he could do to turn Milo sales around.

2. The Brief Statement of Teaching Objectives

The second part of the Case Plan is the brief statement of teaching objectives. Its purpose is to clarify the reasons for writing the case and relates to case origin as discussed in Chapter 3. The opening paragraph can be checked against the teaching objectives to see if there is a match between what the educator desires and what the contact person has provided. This statement of teaching objectives will also clarify for the cooperating organization why the case is being written.

After identifying for which course the case is intended and the type of student normally encountered in this course, the reasons why this case might be considered useful need to be given.

A simple and effective way of explaining the teaching objectives is to tie them to the analytical, conceptual and presentation dimensions of the Case Difficulty Cube as illustrated in Exhibit 5-4.

Exhibit 5-4
THE BRIEF STATEMENT OF TEACHING OBJECTIVES

Analytical Dimension

The student should be able to develop the following skills:
- Identify a problem/issue/decision or opportunity
- Evaluate a decision already taken
- Analyze a problem or issue
- Develop decision criteria
- Develop and evaluate alternatives
- Generate an action and implementation plan

Conceptual Dimension

The student should be able to understand and apply the following:
- Theory(ies)
- Concept(s)
- Technique(s)

Presentation Dimension

The student should be able to:
- Separate relevant from available information
- Specify relevant missing information
- Organize information logically
- Develop appropriate assumptions
- Practice data retrieval

The Delbar case intentions and teaching objectives follow:

This case is intended for an introductory course in marketing. The normal participant is a junior manager who takes the course on a part-time basis and has little or no prior exposure to the theoretical side of marketing.

On the analytical dimension, the problem will be stated but no solutions provided. Thus, students will be expected to analyze the data and generate alternatives, decision criteria and an action and implementation plan.

The theoretical concepts in the course focus on the four P's of marketing. This case helps students to develop understanding and skills in dealing with a failed new product introduction.

The case will be well organized, of medium length with little extraneous information allowing students to spend more time on the analytical and conceptual requirements.

3. The Proposed Organization or Outline of the Case by Subtitles

The third part of the Case Plan focuses on organizing the case. Outlining the case by subtitles has several major advantages. It gives an idea of the information flow of the finished case. It also sets a framework within which the data requirements can be assessed. As a result, the data collection and writing stages will be more orderly and easier to execute.

The usual shape of a case in outline form can be represented as a cone standing vertically on its point. The shape relates to a narrowing down or focusing process, rather than the amount of information to be collected at each stage (see Exhibit 5-5).

The Opening Paragraph

As shown in Exhibit 5-5, the opening paragraph forms the eyepiece or lens to the case and sits on top of the cone.

General Company Background

The first subtitle following the opening paragraph could be background, company or the name of the organization. Frequently used other subtitles in this early part of the case include: company or organization history, industry and/or company overview, major product(s)/service(s), the organization's competitive premise, competition, financial overview, organization, geographical coverage, the parent company, business units, or subsidiaries.

Exhibit 5-5
PROPOSED CASE OUTLINE BY SUBTITLES

- The Opening Paragraph
- General Company Background
- Specific Area of Interest
- Specific Problem or Decision
- Alternatives
- Conclusion

For the sample Brazilian case the first subtitle chosen was: Delbar.

Specific Area of Interest

Typically, the next major subtitle starts to focus the case on the major function or part of the organization in which the key decision maker works. For many cases, the decision, problem or opportunity lies in a particular department or function of the organization. For example, the decision may be in marketing, accounting, finance, production, human resources, information systems or some other area of the organization. Additional subtitle options in this section may include: the history of the function, recent changes, relations with other departments, main responsibilities, challenges of the function and staffing.

An additional subtitle often used as part of this area in the case deals with the personal background of the decision maker and other key people in the case. Optional subtitles may include: the name of the person, the position of the person, personal background or personal history.

For the Delbar case the second subtitle was: The Marketing Area.

Specific Issue, Decision, Problem or Opportunity

Further focusing takes place by concentrating on the specific issue or decision at hand. The context has been established for the contributing organization and the area within which the decision is placed. The number of potential subtitles under this section will vary with each case. Samples could include: the project, the project schedule, the new product launch, the production process, the re-organization plan, the bank's offer, the financing plan, the system start-up, the equipment installation, the customer complaint, the accident and the merger proposal. This process of narrowing in as the case progresses can be compared to subsequent shots with a camera with a zoom lens. Starting with a wide angle shot, subsequent shots zoom in on the subject under different sub-titles.

Additional titles may delineate various aspects of the issue. These subtitles might well outline a time frame (for example: Week 1, Week 2 and so on) or they might suggest an event sequence (for example: design, prototype, pilot run and production run).

For the Delbar case, the three subtitles chosen for this segment of the case were: Milo, Milo Launch and Milo Sales Results.

Alternatives

Most important decisions normally involve a choice among two or more alternatives. The case writer chooses whether to provide none, some or all of these alternatives considered within the contributing organization. The educational purpose and the decision frame cut choice will dictate how many alternatives to include. Alternatives may be identified by capital letters (Alternative A), or numbers (Alternative 1), or by the type of decisions (such as The Make Alternative or The Buy Alternative), or by the origin of the alternative (such as Campbell's Proposal and Williamson's Proposal).

In the Delbar case, the case writer did not want to provide any alternatives and hence no subtitles were needed in this section.

Conclusion

Every case requires an ending. For some case writers the last subtitle can simply be the word Conclusion. Often, the case just ends with a paragraph or two following the section on alternatives without a separate heading. Since the ending often contains deadline information, other subtitles like The Next Meeting, The Task Force Schedule, The Customer's Expectations, The Deadline, and The Board of Directors Meeting are typical options.

For the Delbar case the case writer decided not to use a separate subtitle for the conclusion.

Therefore, in the Delbar case, the case writer decided to use only five subtitles. These were: Delbar, The Marketing Area, Milo, Milo Launch, and Milo Sales Forecasts and Results.

4. Data Requirements List

The most difficult part of the Case Plan deals with the listing of data requirements under each subtitle. In the first place, it is already a challenge for most case writers to visualize what their final case will look like in terms of major building blocks by identifying the subtitles. Secondly, it is difficult to identify just how much information needs to be included in the case to meet the teaching objectives. Nagging in the back of the case writer's head may also be the worry that the information may not be available in real life. It is probably more appealing to go data collecting "shooting from the hip" so to speak. Nevertheless, it is most important to go through this fourth step carefully to help avoid misunderstandings and to facilitate data collection, provisional release and the subsequent writing process.

A case writer should not ask for all available information in the company in hopes of finding the relevant and interesting parts later. The data requirements list is a custom designed, tailor made specification for the necessary information that will allow students to achieve the educational objectives intended through their preparation and discussion of the case. The data requirements section of Exhibit 5-6 has two components: (A) data already known from prior research and initial contact and (B) data to be gathered subsequently.

Exhibit 5-6
THE ORGANIZATION OF THE CASE AND DATA REQUIREMENTS

Case Outline	Data Requirements	
	(A) Data Already Available	(B) Additional Data to be Gathered
The Opening Paragraph		
General Company Background	1. 2.	1. 2.
Specific Area of Interest	1. 2. 3.	1. 2. 3.
Specific Problem or Decision	1. 2. 3. 4.	1. 2. 3. 4.
Alternatives (Optional)	1. 2. 3.	1. 2. 3.
Conclusion	1. 2.	1. 2.

The data specification should be done so well that another case writer could take the Case Plan and complete the case just the way the original case writer intended. Thus, it is not sufficiently precise to ask for financial statements. Are these the income statement and balance sheet for the latest year available or for the past three years? Do they include all of the auditors' comments and explanations or not?

It is not sufficiently precise to ask for an organization chart. Is this a chart showing all the major holdings of the parent organization? Or is it one showing the top management structure, including or excluding the names of the individuals holding the various positions? Or is it a chart showing the organization of the finance department at head office?

It is useful to start with the absolutely vital information without which the case would be useless. Then, if part of the purpose of the case is to separate relevant information from less relevant data, the decision as to what else to include can be made later.

If the information-specifying task is done well, it makes it much easier for the focal person in the case to indicate: 1) whether the information was available to the decision maker at the time the issue was considered; 2) whether the participating organization is willing to provide such information for the case; and 3) whether the suggested disguise is appropriate.

Therefore, the task is to specify under each of the major subtitles what information still needs to be acquired and what has already been obtained before and during the initial contact.

A key argument for using cases in an educational program is to allow students to make decisions or solve problems in a specific real life context. There is no one solution that is absolutely superior to all others for a particular type of problem. If an organization is losing money, cost-cutting measures may work wonders in one organization, while increasing revenues may be preferable for another. Therefore, the purpose of providing a case setting is to allow students to develop judgment as to which actions are preferable under the specific circumstances in this case. The information provided to the case reader needs to be sufficient to provide a meaningful context for the decision or issue at stake.

Therefore, the critical question in specifying the data requirements in a Case Plan becomes: for resolving the decision, problem, opportunity or issue under consideration, what does the reader need to know? What are the necessary details about the company or organization as a whole, about the functional area or position, the key decision maker and the issue itself that the student must know to be able to step into the position of the focal person? What is sufficient information to allow someone previously not familiar with this situation to perform a relevant analysis with some confidence and justification and make a reasonable decision?

The following comments concerning data requirements will apply to the major subtitle areas of any case as well as the Delbar case example under consideration.

General Company Background

This section tells the reader in broad outline some relevant facts about the organization as a whole. What products or services are offered? What industry is it part of? What is its history? Where is the organization located? What size is it and financially where does it stand? This section is intended to place subsequent information in context. For example, whether the company is large or small and whether it is financially well off or not may seriously affect the range of alternatives which can reasonably be considered as pertinent to the decision or problem at hand. Standard information under the heading of General Company Background or its equivalent includes information about the location, number of employees, financial strength, product or service offerings, growth history, future growth potential and competitive premise.

Applying the relevance arguments presented above to the Brazilian case example, how much does the reader need to know about the Delbar Company to be able to address the sales problem with Milo? Does the reader need an organization chart, financial statements, history from the origin to the present of the company, the size of the organization in terms of number of employees, the product range, the competition, the industry, how long the president has been in office and what his or her personal background is?

The Brazilian case writer concluded that the minimum desirable information for the general background section for the Delbar case should include:

1. The size of the company in terms of number of employees and total sales volumes.
2. The major product lines produced and sold and their approximate percentage of total sales.
3. The markets the company serves geographically, the total number of clients, and the three major reasons why they purchase from Delbar.
4. The approximate total sales volume of the company and profitability after taxes as a percentage of sales.
5. The ownership of the company.
6. The competitive climate, number of major competitors and their approximate market share.

The Specific Areas of Interest

It is almost always necessary to provide the case reader with information about the area within which the focal person in the case works. What are the major responsibilities of this area within the context of the business as a whole? How many people work in this area? What is the annual budget? How is this area organized? Is it growing, stable or declining in numbers of people and budget? What are the major challenges facing this area? Is there anything special or unique about it?

It is also desirable in most cases to provide some background information about the position held by the key decision maker in the case. What are the main job responsibilities of this position and where does it fit within the organization structure?

Although it is often not essential for the purpose of the case, the personal background of the key decision maker may provide a special touch. Since the normal case assignment is, "If you were in the position of the key decision maker in this case, what would be your analysis and plan of action and why?", the personal background of the actual decision maker is not normally required. However, such a background does give the case reader a chance to see how individuals move into various positions on the organizational ladder.

For the Delbar case, under the Marketing Area subtitle, the case writer requested the following additional information:

1. Key responsibilities of marketing and sales.
2. Number of people in marketing working at head office and elsewhere.
3. The organization of the department showing the split between marketing and sales and to whom the key decision maker in the case reports.
4. The primary channels of distribution used.
5. The primary means of promotion used.
6. The key elements of Delbar's marketing strategy.
7. The major challenges faced in the marketing area.
8. The pricing strategy used.

For the background of the marketing manager, the case writer asked for:

1. Educational background.
2. Number of years with Delbar.

3. Number of jobs held at Delbar and number of years per job.
4. Number of other companies and type of other companies worked for and positions held.

The Specific Decision, Problem, Issue or Opportunity

This section of the case provides the first opportunity to refer to the issue initially mentioned in the opening paragraph. Now the challenge for the case writer becomes to specify the information which, in the case writer's opinion, the decision maker might reasonably have used. Such information will normally include both qualitative and quantitative data relevant to the issue at hand. Included are factual data as well as the opinions of various people involved in the issue. Clearly, such information will range widely depending on the issue, decision, problem or opportunity under consideration.

For the Brazilian case, the case writer divided the issue into three titles: Milo, The Milo Launch, and Milo Sales Forecasts and Results. Under these subtitles the following additional information was requested:

Milo

1. Description of the product and its functionality.
2. Direct and indirect competitive products.
3. The major advantages of Milo over other products.
4. Who developed Milo? When and why?
5. The timing of Milo development.
6. Why did Delbar choose to include Milo in its product line?
7. Who are major customers for Milo?
8. Variable and fixed costs of Milo production and development.

Milo Launch

1. What was the timing of the Milo launch?
2. What promotion was planned for Milo, why and when?
3. What pricing strategy was chosen for Milo and why?

4. What distribution was planned and why?
5. Who developed the launch plan for Milo and when?
6. Key differences between the Milo launch and other products launched by Delbar.

Milo Sales Forecasts and Results

1. Actual Milo sales for the months of August, September and October as well as forecasts for these months.
2. Sales distribution for Milo by geographical region for August, September and October compared to forecasts.
3. Any information about changes from the launch plan that occurred in price, distribution or promotion.
4. Any information about customer feedback on Milo received during the first three months.

Conclusion

Whether or not a case writer decides to use a subtitle for the concluding part of the case, it is normal to write a concluding paragraph. Often, the concluding paragraph is a re-statement of the challenge presented in the opening paragraph and reinforces the sense of urgency faced by the decision maker by reiterating the decision deadline. A well crafted stirring conclusion will inspire the student.

5. The Time Plan

The time plan is the fifth part required to complete the Case Plan. The time plan is the proposed schedule for the key steps in the case writing process (see Exhibit 5-7). It conveys seriousness about deadlines and identifies expectations for both the case writer and the contributing organization.

Normally, the Case Plan portion of the time plan is relatively short, allowing for 48 hours to one week to conclude Phase 1 of the case writing process. It is Phase 2 (as identified in Exhibit 2-3), comprising the data collection and writing phases, that tends to be longer.

Exhibit 5-7
THE TIME PLAN

ACTIVITY	DATE
Case Plan completion	_____
Case Plan sent to contributing organization	_____
Second interview with contributing organization	_____
Provisional release	_____
Data collection	_____
Rough draft of case	_____
Preliminary teaching note	_____
Edited case	_____
Case released	_____

It is useful to let the case contact person know that the Case Plan is simply that, a plan that will be revised to incorporate changes suggested by the case contact. For example, data gathering may depend on the availability of certain individuals. While the case writer can fully control the Case Plan preparation, the writing of the case and the teaching note development, both sides are involved in data collection. And release is fully under the case contact's control. Thus, the time plan, whether accepted as proposed or modified to suit the needs of both parties, does become a commitment to develop the case to a target deadline. In this sense, the writing of the case can and should be managed as a project, with a beginning, scheduled milestones and an end point.

The completed Case Plan becomes the tool for obtaining provisional release.

PROVISIONAL RELEASE

Provisional release is the "green light" to proceed to Phase 2 of the case writing process (see Exhibit 2-3) and it is the main topic during the second interview. The Case Plan is the key to obtaining a provisional release. The Case Plan shows the proposed disguise and tests the understanding of preliminary information given during the first interview. The case writer can say,

> Up to now, I have not committed a large amount of time and effort to this case. If you have any reservations at all about the correctness of the issue, the availability of the information or your willingness to cooperate on this, let's call it off now and there are no hard feelings. On the other hand, my assumption is that, if you agree to proceed on the basis of this plan, I can expect something in return. That is, if I collect the information as listed and write the case as I show I intend to do here, I expect you will release it. I would like a provisional release now because both you and I are going to commit time and effort after this meeting to complete the case.

It is good practice to e-mail, fax or mail the Case Plan in advance of the second interview to allow the case contact to examine the plan at leisure and discuss it with others, if necessary. A well-prepared plan may not even require a formal second interview and data collection can proceed directly based on a telephone call, e-mail or fax confirmation of the proposed plan.

If changes to the Case Plan are requested by the case contact, then it is good practice to send the revised version of the Case Plan as quickly as possible along with the following message:

> Please find enclosed (attached or appended) the new Case Plan revised as per your suggestions. This revision will be our commitment to proceed as planned and, unless I hear otherwise from you, I am looking forward to working with you to write this case. It is my understanding that if I execute this Case Plan as now agreed, you will release the final version of the case for educational purposes. I am sure this will be a good case and much appreciated by my students and I thank you for your assistance to date.

On the assumption that the Case Plan has been accepted and a provisional release granted, it is now possible to proceed to the next stage of the case writing process: data collection.

CHAPTER SIX

data collection

When the case writer has obtained the provisional release, the stage is set for data collection. This step entails gathering the necessary information, as identified on the data requirements list of the Case Plan. If the data requirements list was well done, data collection should be a matter of filling in the blanks. In reality, however, data collection presents some challenges.

Potential data sources are:

1. outside the organization in published or unpublished form;

2. inside the organization in written form, some readily accessible and some highly confidential and difficult to obtain;

3. inside the organization in unwritten form. This information may also be subdivided into easy and difficult to collect. Part of the difficulty may stem from the researcher's inability to identify the proper source. A secondary difficulty lies in obtaining the information, even after the source has been correctly identified.

Some information is not available in any form. The case writer then may state in the case that this information was not available.

Since the data to be collected had to be available to the focal person at the time of the case, this person becomes the key source for the information to be collected. And the primary means of collection becomes the personal interview. Therefore, a significant part of this chapter will focus on the interviewing process, including potential pitfalls and difficulties.

Comments on data security, confidentiality and organization for writing will conclude this chapter.

THE PERSONAL INTERVIEW

Although substantial information may be available in printed or electronic form, the case writer still depends on one or more personal interviews for a significant portion of data collection.

The personal interview is a common research tool and the case writer is advised to review any of the standard texts on interviewing. The purpose of the personal interview is to discover and collect the pertinent facts and opinions about the case as efficiently and unobtrusively as possible. In every case, it is essential that the case writer documents accurately the story line and decision frame as well as the relevant action trigger and background information.

Effective interviewing comprises more than just asking questions and securing answers. If it were that simple, the case writer could simply send the data requirements list to the contributing organization and ask to have it filled out and returned. Good interviewing requires the case writer to be there in person because the answer to a question may be unexpected or incomplete, requiring additional probing or clarification.

Preparation

It is good practice for the case writer to prepare well for each interview so as to minimize the time and to maximize the benefit of the interview. The preparation focuses on the data to be collected, as specified in the data requirements list, and the interview with the key person. Before each interview, the case writer should review carefully all material gathered in published form, such as press releases, annual reports, web pages and magazine articles; or in unpublished form, such as internal memos, e-mail messages and confidential reports. The notes from the first interview and the Case Plan provide the context for any subsequent interview.

Carefully worded questions posed in a logical order are appreciated by busy managers. These questions should normally focus on the items of the data requirements list not available from other sources. Detailed and specific lists of questions prepared ahead of time ensure to-the-point interviews where no time is being wasted. Therefore, the case writer must be prepared to guide the conversation with intelligent questions, but not to pre-plan the interview to such an extent that it prevents the manager from giving any unsolicited ideas or pertinent data.

Interviewing Rules

Following is a list of basic rules for conducting effective case writing interviews:

1. *Select the appropriate interviewee*

Normally it is best to interview the key decision maker first and then rely on his or her suggestions as to which other persons should be interviewed to fill in the gaps and necessary details.

Top managers are normally the best sources to provide overall views of their organization and competition. They are more familiar with legal and financial structures and more able to report on the past history and future plans of the company. Middle and lower level managers can be relied upon for the details of daily operations but may be reluctant to answer questions of policy.

It is advisable to stay away from outsiders whose knowledge about the issue of the case may not have been available to the decision maker at the time of the case, unless they are recommended by the manager who will release the case.

2. Establish a rapport with the interviewee

Establishing a good rapport with each interviewee is vital to a successful interview. It is important to create a climate where the case writer feels comfortable in asking questions and the manager is keen to provide answers. The case writer's demeanor affects the outcome. If the case writer is tense and formal, the interview will likely be strained. Most people respond best to an amicable, enthusiastic, relaxed but courteous approach.

Initially, taking some time to talk about topics, such as family, sports or the weather helps to set the tone for communication and trust. Case writers should give the interviewee time to become comfortable with them as well as to assess their competence and credibility.

Confirming how much time has been set aside for the interview will show the case researcher's respect for the manager's busy schedule and help keep the interview within the set time limits.

3. Explain or clarify the case writer's role

Just because a provisional release has been granted, the case writer should not assume that each interviewee will know and understand the nature of the undertaking. When the case writer is introduced to an interviewee different from the initial contact, it is important not only to explain the purpose of the interview but also to specify his or her role as case writer. He or she should explain that the objective is to collect facts and opinions about a situation for educational purposes, not to assess the management views or past decisions. It should also be stressed that no information will be seen and used by others without a formal review of the case and release by the company. This assurance should reduce any feeling of threat or anxiety, especially if the interviewee knows the case writer in another capacity, such as a consultant or a professor.

4. Listen carefully to the interviewee

It has been said that the success of the interview depends on how much the interviewer can keep his or her mouth shut. Concentrated listening benefits not only the listener but also the speaker. A case researcher who does not pay full attention to what the manager is saying will impact negatively on the quality of the information provided. Active listening requires concentration and is a skill that the case writer must cultivate.

5. Remain objective

The case researcher must absorb and comprehend what the respondent is saying while remaining objective. He or she must refrain from expressing feelings, thoughts or opinions; from giving any advice; and, above all, from arguing. Such restraint is sometimes difficult for academics.

The case writer must also clearly understand and be able to distinguish the difference between facts and opinions. Facts can be verified. Opinions can only be included in the case if they are attributed explicitly to someone. It is not the case writer's job to establish the truth as far as opinions are concerned or to express his or her own opinions.

6. Assess data accuracy, completeness and consistency

The case writer must constantly evaluate the adequacy of the information he or she receives for fulfilling the objectives of the case and implementing the Case Plan. The case writer may tactfully call the manager's attention to apparent inconsistencies, contradictions or omissions.

If something is not clear to the case writer, it will not be clear to the students reading the case either. Clarity and accuracy of information is therefore key. To check understanding, it is useful to restate frequently by summarizing what has been said earlier or to ask for clarification. For example, the case writer may say, "Let me just see if I got this straight: Did you say that …?" or "Am

I missing something in the sequence of events here? First this happened and then what followed immediately afterward?" Probing is a good tactic for obtaining needed elaboration or clarification of information. It should always be done in a direct and non-confronting way.

Note Taking

Note taking during and immediately following the interview is essential for accuracy. Moreover, it is time effective and less intimidating than tape recording.

A useful technique consists of jotting down major points or key words during the interview and filling in all the details as soon as possible afterwards. One should not try to write everything down. Excessive note taking gets in the way of listening, slows down and disturbs the flow of the interview. It is useful to develop a system of abbreviations and symbols for frequently used words. Experienced case writers often develop their own shorthand style that only they can read. However, they should complete their notes soon after the interview or even they may not know what their notes mean.

Cases can be dull and quotes will enliven them. Quotes are a good way to express opinions and attitudes, show authority, convey authenticity and add variety. Upon hearing a good quote, it is important to record the words verbatim. This is one instance that calls for interrupting the interviewee and checking on the exact words of the quote.

Recording and Videotaping

It is possible to use a tape recorder in case writing interviews. However, many case writers prefer not to because of the time, cost and trouble of listening to, retrieving and transcribing pertinent data. Moreover, it can inhibit the interviewee and hamper the quality of the information. If a case writer wishes to record an interview, permission should be obtained first and, of course, he or she must be thoroughly familiar with the equipment.

It is also possible to videotape interviews as well as the actual premises of the organization. Some cases lend themselves to this type of visual recording which can be an effective teaching aid in the classroom.

Collecting Other Materials

It is often useful to ask for samples, photos, brochures, company videos and promotional or other materials. While some of this material may be used as exhibits in the case, others can be used as teaching aids to enrich class discussion. Bringing into the classroom the actual product described in the case adds reality and credibility.

Subsequent Data Gathering

At the conclusion of a face-to-face interview, it is good practice for the case researcher to ask permission to call back or use electronic mail to fill in possible gaps.

It is recommended not to call, fax or e-mail the manager each time the researcher has a question but rather to accumulate these questions until the end of the data collection process. Telephone interviews work best for questions that require simple or clear-cut answers. The case writer should be well prepared for these follow-up interviews, give a rough estimate of the proposed call duration, get to the various points quickly and record the answers carefully.

DATA COLLECTION PITFALLS AND DIFFICULTIES

As in any plan implementation, the process is not always straight forward. The original Case Plan may not fit the actual on-site situation, once the researcher starts digging beneath the surface. Unexpected events require other information which may not be readily available. The time needed to obtain information may surpass original estimates. Sometimes, too much information may be available and the problem becomes a sorting one. Occasionally, interviewees may be uncooperative or unavailable. When such difficulties occur, the case writer must strive to satisfy the needs of both the educational institution and the contributing organization.

Questionable Reliability and Validity of Data

A case writer visiting the contributing organization is often exposed to new surroundings. Some questions that may come to mind are, "Is what I am observing actually a normal occurrence?" or "Are the people only putting on a big show for me?" or "Are things really the way they say they are?"

There are times when information becomes distorted and it is difficult to understand why. Information passed from employee to employee via the grapevine is frequently incorrect. A case writer can try to substantiate it by using different sources. On the other hand, a question could be asked to which a number of different answers may be given and it could be difficult to select the correct one. The case writer may make this choice based on incomplete information if an interviewee intentionally or unintentionally excludes a key fact. However, the case writer may be to blame if he or she is acting on an erroneous assumption made during the interview to make limited data fit into the Case Plan.

When writing a current case, the case writer should not, of course, be affecting the decision making process. It may happen that with each new visit to the organization, the information appears to change or evolve. There can almost be a feeling that the case writer's questions are causing the answers to change. The best way to avoid this type of problem is to set the case story line and decision frame cuts slightly earlier (see Chapter 4).

With cases set in the past, the case writer must deal with the respondent's inability to recall accurately certain types of information. As time tends to distort memories, the case writer always has to assess the reporting reliability. The more distant in time the case is, the more forgetting will be a barrier to data collection. Some managers may also be tempted to justify or rationalize their actions or decisions by information or ideas gained after they acted but which should not be part of the case. Writing cases about more current decisions will prevent some of these difficulties.

Data may be affected internally and externally by the impressions, assumptions and biases of the case writer or the person being interviewed.

If the interviewee does not have the proper authority to release information, he or she may say something he or she should not or else falsify the facts.

When unsure of the reliability and validity of data, the interviewer may verify the material from other sources, spoken and written where possible, or ask the same questions of the same person but in a different manner.

Unpredictable Factors

Sometimes observations may be affected by actions or events beyond the case writer's control. Unpredictable factors can influence the outcome of the interviewing process, such as the personality, position and authority of the person being interviewed and whether he or she is busy or relatively free. These factors may also be totally external, like a merger, an acquisition offer or a strike. The interviewer has little choice but to display flexibility and adapt to these unpredictable factors.

Uncooperative Interviewee

For all kinds of reasons, some of which may be beyond the case writer's control, an interviewee may be uncooperative. The answers to questions may be evasive or too brief for the researcher to obtain adequate information. Or worse, the interviewee may be too fearful to yield any pertinent information.

Key barriers to cooperation may be conflicting demands for time (the interviewee would rather be devoting time to something else) and ego threat (the interviewee tends to withhold information which may threaten self-esteem, like the acknowledgment of a judgment error or a bad decision). If it is a question of bad timing, the case writer may suggest rescheduling the interview at a more appropriate time. If it appears to be a question of ego threat, the case writer should try to appease the interviewee, establish a better rapport and reiterate the non-judgmental role of the case writer. It nothing works, it may be best to find a more cooperative interviewee if possible.

Inappropriate Roles for the Case Writer

Despite all the case writer's best efforts to establish clearly the nature of his or her role, some interviewees may still push the case writer to assume other roles. A common one is the role of confidant. Sometimes, managers, especially at the top of the hierarchy, are lonely. They welcome the opportunity to share and discuss their problems and dilemmas with a confidential and neutral party. This may generate good case material but at the price of lengthy digressions. However, as flattering as it may be to be asked, the case writer must resist adopting the roles of counselor, advisor or mediator.

DATA SECURITY AND CONFIDENTIALITY

The responsibility for the control and use of collected data lies with the case writer. He or she must take measures to ensure data security.

It is crucial that all divulged information remains confidential until final release has been secured. After receiving the release, it is good practice to shred all unused sensitive information or return it to the organization. Maintaining good relations with the contributing organization in implementing the Case Plan is the guiding principle of case data collection and should never be jeopardized.

DATA ORGANIZATION

Once the case writer is satisfied that all necessary data have been collected, the task is to organize this information to facilitate the drafting of the case. The case writer may have pieces and bits on specific items of the data requirements list buried in various documents and interview notes. Starting to write without spending the time to sort systematically all the collected material may result in the loss of important pieces of information. Having a way of knowing where all the information pertaining to each item of the data requirements list is located saves a lot of time and frustration.

A good way to deal with a long and complex case is to assign a numerical and/or alphabetical code to each single item of the data requirements list. The case writer may have a special code for teaching note material, as some information that has been collected may be analytical in nature and better suited for inclusion in the teaching note than the case itself.

Next it is a question of grouping together all the documents or interview notes marked with the same code; for example, A 5 for competition under the General Company Background subtitle, or D 2 for the second alternative considered in the case.

This data sorting system is an excellent way to prepare for the often daunting task of actual case writing, because this writing can be done in small focused parts. The case writer is now ready to draft the case.

CHAPTER SEVEN

case writing and preliminary teaching note

The actual writing of the case consists of fleshing out the Case Plan with the information gathered in the data collection phase. Some case writers say their major challenge lies in trying to understand the story line and crafting a detailed Case Plan. Others say their challenge begins with the writing of the case once the data are collected.

Regardless of which camp a case writer sides with, the actual writing of the case involves four steps: (1) writing a rough draft, (2) preparing a preliminary teaching note, (3) revising the rough draft, and (4) editing the case.

WRITING A ROUGH DRAFT

The Case Plan augmented by the additional information gathered in the data collection phase provides the framework for the rough draft of a case. In the Case Plan, the major decisions regarding the organization of the case, what to include and where, have already been made. The rough drafting process consists of developing the sentences and paragraphs according to the suggested outline. Since there is likely to be more than one rough draft, it is better to concentrate on putting the right information in the right place in the case and not to worry too much about the grammar at this stage. In rough drafting, consideration is given to the number of paragraphs needed under each of the subtitles of the Case Plan, and what information to include in each paragraph. The case writer decides how extensive the coverage needs to be for each point and in what sequence.

The information to include in each paragraph depends on the level of detail required to describe the story line. For example, consider a paragraph in a case where a manufacturing company has received a complaint from a major customer regarding damaged goods shipped by the manufacturer's distributor. Relevant details in such a paragraph would include how long the goods were at the distributor's facility; how they were stored; how they were shipped; what kind of records were kept at the factory and at the distributor's facility; and what the performance history of the distributor was.

Furthermore, consideration needs to be given as to how each point will be made. Alternatives here include narrating the case facts, providing a chronology of events, attributing opinions to people in the organization, using quotes, and/or putting the necessary information in the form of an exhibit.

For example, the following two options are different possibilities for the first paragraph in the Organization Background section of the Brazilian case example presented in Chapter 5.

> **Option #1.** Delbar was founded by the grandfather of the current president in 1965. He had been laid off by his employer and decided to start a business on his own. He bought several pieces of second-hand, general purpose equipment to produce replacement parts for automotive and equipment maintenance shops in the Curitiba area in Brazil. High quality and fast service won him many clients; and by the time of his death in 1985, the company had expanded to about 170 employees.
>
> **Option #2.** Delbar, located in Curitiba, Brazil, about 500 kilometers south of San Paulo, employed about 700 people. It had two core businesses. One was the quick response machining

of small volume parts for the automotive and equipment repair market. The other, accounting for about 60 percent of the total sales volume, included the distribution of maintenance, repair and operating supplies. The company had 28 branches located in all major industrial centers in Brazil.

Both paragraphs are useful under the same subtitle, but only one can be first.

In writing the first rough draft, it is generally better to include too much information rather than too little. For most case writers overwriting is not a problem, especially when writing about an organization's background or the current competitive environment. Ample data for these sections of the case outline are likely to be readily available, and it is easy to write numerous pages of background information. The real question is, how much of this information is relevant to the issue and appropriate for the story line of the case?

The challenging part of rough drafting the case comes in the specific area of interest and the specific issue or decision sections. Here, case writers must be clear about the story line: who was involved, what were the relevant data, how did events happen, where, and when? There is a tendency for case writers to leave out relevant data. Either the case writer has not asked the right question(s), and/or has not totally understood the data provided or the teaching/learning objectives of the case. Careful crafting of the Case Plan and collecting the appropriate data makes writing the rough draft considerably easier.

Rough Drafting Conventions

Case writing follows a number of conventions. Four of these apply to writing the rough draft of a case. Other case writing conventions apply to the editing process and are covered later in this chapter.

Past Tense

Cases are normally written in the past tense, third person, except for direct quotes and when presenting exhibit and appendix information. This convention reflects the reality that by the time a student reads the case, all of the facts of the case situation are in the past. Using the present tense implies that the case is fictional. New case writers often resist this convention, believing that the past tense makes all the facts appear dead. Quotes are a good way to add life to a case. Practice in presenting the facts in different ways also helps. For example, rather than writing: "Delbar was a medium sized company which employed about 700 people", we can write: "The president of Delbar said, 'We now have 700 employees, quite a change from when my grandfather died in 1985 when we had only 170.'" Furthermore, cases written in the past tense prevent the mixing of the tenses and retain their usefulness for teaching longer than cases written in the present tense.

Facts, Opinions, Attributions

The relevant facts that were available to the decision maker have to be included in the case, as identified in the data requirements list of the Case Plan. If certain facts were not available to the decision maker, the case normally should say so. For example: "Mr. Roberts did not know the equipment replacement cost." Since a case writer is just reporting the company's story, his or her opinions are not to be included. Any opinions expressed in the case must be attributed to the people mentioned in the case.

Exhibits and Appendixes

Exhibits are an economical way to present data and to provide the raw materials for developing student analytical skills. Tables of numbers, charts, forms, graphs, diagrams, pictures and maps are typical examples of the kinds of data displayed in exhibits. Exhibits typically come after the text of the case and are numbered consecutively in the order of their reference in the case text. All exhibits must be referenced in the text. Exhibits normally have three lines in their title: the name of the case, the exhibit number and the exhibit title.

The normal assumption is that the exhibit information comes from company records and hence it is not necessary to provide a specific reference to that effect. If the data or materials are not from company records, a specific reference to the source of the information is given at the bottom of each exhibit. Information in the exhibits is presented in the tense used by the company and may be reproduced in full, in extracts or in summary form.

Sometimes, case writers construct exhibits based on the data collected. Examples include process flow diagrams, simplified organization charts or highlights of the historical financial performance. Sometimes case writers deliberately leave out certain data in an exhibit or only partially complete the information in an exhibit, because students are expected to complete the exhibit as part of their analysis. For example, an exhibit may show the cycle times for an operator tending three of four machines and students need to calculate the fourth machine cycle. An exhibit may show only the line item analysis of the financial performance, and students need to complete the year-over-year analysis. The extent to which an exhibit is a simplification, extraction, summary, partial representation or a complete reprint of the company document will affect the position of the case on the Case Difficulty Cube. The principle in preparing exhibits is to provide useful information to allow meaningful analyses or calculations that are in line with the teaching objectives of the case.

Appendixes are used to provide materials that are complementary or useful but not an integral part of the case. Sometimes appendix information can be a substitute for a specific reading that might otherwise be assigned to accompany a case. Sometimes an appendix is used to provide some descriptive information regarding an industry, a process or a government regulation. Appendixes normally are placed after the exhibits at the end of the case, are labeled A, B, C, and placed consecutively in order of their reference in the case. Information in an appendix is normally presented in the same tense as the original. The source of information presented in an appendix must be acknowledged.

Case Length

There are no particular conventions or rules on how long cases should be. The shortest case is the opening paragraph from the Case Plan. Long cases are those exceeding 20 pages of text including exhibits and appendixes.

Case length is dictated by student preparation time, the learning objectives and the position on the Case Difficulty Cube. Longer cases may be justified by the complexity of the situation. For example, a case about a company trying to develop a strategic response to a competitor's actions in a global industry may require extensive data to help students develop a clear perspective and understanding of the situation. A case at the third level of difficulty on the presentation dimension of the Case Difficulty Cube is likely to be a long one as well.

It is easy to write long cases. Case writers often start to write, without careful positioning on the Case Difficulty Cube. They then provide lots of information on the General Background section of the case, simply because the data are readily available. The case quickly becomes 20 pages or more and the case writer gets committed to the words – all the words. Cutting back the information becomes difficult.

There are some veteran case writers who say, "If you can't write the case in less than 15 pages, it probably isn't worth writing." We think cases longer than 10 pages plus three or four exhibits require a lot of reading time as part of student preparation time. In *Learning with Cases*, we suggest that instructors should expect no more than an hour and a half to two hours of individual preparation on a case. With long cases, students do not have sufficient time to read and prepare the case. And when they stop reading and preparing properly, they become more and more reluctant to participate in class. Instructors, in turn, become more and more frustrated with the lack of student enthusiasm and preparation. This negative spiral destroys effective case teaching and learning.

Our preference is for case writers to write short cases. A "short read, long think" case has a much greater chance of success than a "long read, no think" case.

PREPARING A PRELIMINARY TEACHING NOTE

The purpose of preparing a preliminary teaching note after rough drafting the case is to check the completeness and accuracy of the information presented. It is essential that the case contain the right information. A preliminary teaching note typically has seven headings: Case Title, Opening Paragraph or Case Synopsis, Teaching Objectives, Immediate Issue(s), Basic Issue(s), Suggested Student Assignment and Case Analysis. Appendix 3 is an example of a preliminary teaching note.

The first three headings and their contents are included in the preliminary teaching note primarily for reviewing their congruence with the Case Plan.

Case Title

Now that the rough draft of the case has been prepared, is the case title as proposed in the Case Plan still appropriate? Would a different title be better? Remember, case titles are intended to be neutral (see Chapter 5).

Opening Paragraph

Is the opening paragraph in the Case Plan still appropriate for the rough draft? If the opening paragraph has changed, can the questions in the opening paragraph check list still be successfully answered? Remember, students will be asked to answer similar questions as part of their preparation using the Short Cycle Process (see *Learning with Cases*, Chapter 3).

Teaching Objectives

Are the teaching objectives as proposed in the Case Plan (see Chapter 5) still appropriate? If not, how have they changed and why?

The next two headings in the preliminary teaching note address the context of the case and the content of the course.

Immediate Issue(s)

From the story line and decision time frame presented in the case, is it possible to state the specific issue(s), challenge(s), decision(s), opportunity(ies) facing the decision maker in the case? Is it possible to identify from the context of the case information what the decision maker needs to do? The immediate issues are the ones the decision maker needs to resolve and the ones the student will have to deal with in the context of the case (see *Learning with Cases*, Chapter 3).

Basic Issue(s)

The basic issues refer to the instructor's reasons for using the case in the course as identified in the Case Origin Grid. Basic issues are the ones the student will generalize from and apply to other contexts and situations. Considering the course or program for which the case is being written, is it possible to identify the basic or underlying issue(s), principle(s), concept(s) or technique(s) that comprise the subject matter of the course (see *Learning with Cases*, Chapter 3)?

The last two headings typically included in a preliminary teaching note are the suggested student assignment questions and the answers to these questions that the information as presented in the rough draft allows.

Suggested Student Assignment

In preparing the suggested student assignment, the case writer now takes an instructor's perspective. "If I were to assign this rough draft of the case to my students to prepare for class discussion, what would I ask them to think about?" The standard case assignment question asks the student to take the position of the focal person and deal with the immediate issue(s) in the case. For example, "Please put yourself in the position of Mrs. Wheeler. What is your analysis of this situation, your decision and your proposed action plan?" or "In the position of Mrs. Wheeler, what would you do and why?" would be common case analysis assignment questions. Additional assignment questions can be more specifically related to the content of the course. Examples are questions like, "What is your analysis of the production process?" "What is the profitability of the proposed investment?" and "Who are the key stakeholders in this case and how will each react to the proposal?"

If uncertainty or confusion exists regarding the appropriateness of the suggested student assignment questions, the case writer should check with the case supervisor.

Case Analysis

In the case analysis section of the preliminary teaching note, the case writer now takes the student perspective and completes the Short Cycle Process, the Long Cycle Process and the Case Preparation Chart (see *Learning with Cases*, Chapter 3) using the rough draft of the case and the suggested student assignment. Now the task for the case writer is to verify the completeness and accuracy of the rough draft case information with respect to each assignment question. If an adequate answer or position can be developed for each suggested assignment question, then moving on to editing is appropriate. If any of the suggested questions cannot be adequately answered, then the rough draft of the case needs more work or the assignment questions need to be changed or both.

REVISING THE ROUGH DRAFT

Typically, the suggested assignment questions are appropriate but the information provided in the rough draft does not allow for adequate analysis. Five questions help determine whether or not the case contains the right information.

1. What relevant qualitative or quantitative data are missing?
2. Is the information correct?
3. Are the descriptions and explanations clear?
4. Does the case have too much irrelevant information?
5. Has the case writer included personal judgments and included his or her own analysis?

Changes to the rough draft may be required. First, it is sometimes necessary to go back to the contact person to collect more information. For example, if one of the teaching objectives of a case is to apply the notion of the learning curve and students are asked to make decisions on scheduling plant capacity, and information on standards, volumes and production times is missing, it would be useful to collect it.

Using the data already collected, the case writer often needs to clarify, reposition, restate or add more information. Examples here include: the story line is incomplete, the process description needs more clarity, an exhibit showing key players would be helpful, the numbers are not correct.

There is a tendency for case writers to include too much information, especially in the background section of the case. The irrelevance of this information may become evident while completing the preliminary teaching note.

Case writers are often tempted to pass judgments because they wish to interpret the case facts. If such an interpretation reflects an opinion of a person in the contributing organization, proper attribution should be made. Otherwise, such interpretations should be deleted. Sometimes case writers also provide some of their own analysis in the case that students should do during their preparation. Such analyses should be left out.

Answering the above five questions with respect to the information contained in each section of the case is a good way to ensure that the right information is in the right place. Finding another person willing to review the rough draft and to offer feedback on his or her Short and Long Cycle Process analyses can also be very valuable.

It is normal to prepare two or three successive rough drafts of a case. Re-drafting cases requires persistence on the part of a case writer, but pays high dividends.

EDITING THE CASE

Case writers can take a measure of interim satisfaction when the case is ready for editing. The end is in sight. A new case is imminent. Yet, this stage is not the time to lose focus or concern for quality. The professional presentation of a case adds credibility and helps to capture the reader's attention.

The Nine C's Case Editing Checklist

Nine words, each starting with the letter C, form the case editing checklist: Congruence, Completeness, Consistency, Correctness, Conciseness, Clarity, Control, Coherence and Convention. The first three of these words focus on the content of the case itself.

Congruence

Are the descriptions and data regarding products, services, processes or systems terminology in agreement with those of the actual organization, especially if these data are disguised?

Completeness

Has the decision maker's story as well as the company's story been sufficiently told? Are there any gaps or omissions remaining in the story line?

Consistency

Is the information logically and accurately presented throughout the case? Is the disguise, if used, compatible and applied uniformly to the company information?

The next five C words apply to language and grammar. Case information must be presented in the generally accepted form and usage of the language used. In our context, it is the English language, and there are numerous reference texts available to assist in this part of the editing task.

Correctness

Is the past tense used throughout the case? Are the words spelled correctly? Are the grammar and punctuation correct? Are the exhibit and appendix titles in the standard format?

Conciseness

Would some information appearing in the case body be better presented in the form of an exhibit? Can a single phrase be substituted for a whole sentence and can a single word be substituted for a phase? Can a more succinct phase or a single word be used to capture an idea? These are typical questions to ask in trying to present the case information in more concise ways.

Clarity

Are the words chosen precise and likely to be clearly understood? Are the words commonly used in everyday conversation? Are there words that are vague and open to misinterpretation? For example, the pronouns "this" or "it" must refer to a specific noun. Is the writing unnecessarily cluttered with jargon – complicated or unfamiliar terms – and idioms or colloquialisms? For example, the following sentences contain English idioms and terms that may not be clearly understood: "Tom felt he would be going out on a limb in making such a recommendation." "Bill believed he had been hung out to dry." "The traffic jam was growing due to the accident and the usual rubber-necking." The idioms "going out on a limb" and "hung out to dry" mean respectively "taking a risk" and "isolated." The colloquial term "rubber-necking" means vehicle drivers are slowing down to look at the accident. Given a readership that can go considerably beyond native language readers, idiomatic and jargon-laden language should be avoided. Occasionally, when colloquial phrases or idioms add color and interest to the case, they should be noted by quotation marks and accompanied by a footnote explaining the meaning. Plain, short, everyday words in the English language make cases easier to read.

Control

Are the subtitles appropriately chosen? Do the paragraphs adequately develop and frame ideas? Does the first sentence of the paragraph contain the main point? Does the last sentence of the paragraph add closure to the idea being developed? Are the paragraphs logically grouped under each subtitle?

Coherence

Have appropriate words or phrases been chosen to link sentences and parts of sentences? Are there logical transitions between ideas in the paragraphs and between the proceeding paragraphs? Linking words and phrases, such as however, consequently, furthermore, by contrast, on the other hand, and as a result of, help make sentences and paragraphs clear and coherent.

The last C word addresses commonly accepted practice in case writing.

Conventions

Some case writing conventions have already been introduced in the rough drafting part of the process. There are five more that pertain to editing the case.

1. Case Title, Title Page, Formatting and Coding. Cases normally have a standard title page including the institutional logo or seal, the case title, the author(s), a disclaimer, the copyright statement, the opening few paragraphs of the case and a code number. Exhibit 7-1 is a sample case title page.

The copyright statement shown on Exhibit 7-1 is the standard one for Ivey Business School cases. This statement can appear at the top or at the bottom of the title page. The copyright designation means two things. One, the case should not be reproduced without the permission of the copyright holder. Two, no one, except the case author, can make any changes to the case.

Formatting and coding should be consistent for all cases produced by the institution. Formatting refers to font size and style, heading arrangements, spacing, bolding and title guides for exhibits. Coding refers to the numbering or lettering system that uniquely identifies the case or teaching note. The code number for the case shown in Exhibit 7-1 is 9B00D010. It is a good idea to leave extra-wide margins on each case page. Extra-wide margins make it easier for case readers to make notes and do calculations right on the page.

2. Referencing. When cases contain information from published sources beyond the company records, the source should be footnoted at the bottom of the respective page of the case. When an entire case written under the real name of the company is based on published material from the public record, such as the company's annual report or its financial statements as reported in the business press, a footnote attached to the case title can be used to indicate the source.

Exhibit 7-1
SAMPLE CASE TITLE PAGE

Richard Ivey School of Business
The University of Western Ontario

IVEY

9B00D010

HAILEY KENNEDY

Scott Davies prepared this case under the supervision of Professor Jim Erskine solely to provide material for class discussion. The authors do not intend to illustrate either effective or ineffective handling of a managerial situation. The authors may have disguised certain names and other identifying information to protect confidentiality.

Ivey Management Services prohibits any form of reproduction, storage or transmittal without its written permission. This material is not covered under authorization from CanCopy or any reproduction rights organization. To order copies or request permission to reproduce materials, contact Ivey Publishing, Ivey Management Services, c/o Richard Ivey School of Business, The University of Western Ontario, London, Ontario, Canada, N6A 3K7; phone (519) 661-3208; fax (519) 661-3882; e-mail cases@ivey.uwo.ca.

Copyright © 2000, Ivey Management Services Version: 2000-04-17

On Friday August 25, 2000 Hailey Kennedy, Junior Associate at the Burns-Devon and Partners law firm in Toronto, Canada met with Frank Jones her Managing Partner. He had offered Hailey an excellent opportunity and he wanted her decision by Monday.

BURNS-DEVON AND PARTNERS

Burns-Devon and Partners (Burns-Devon) law firm was at the forefront of business and legal developments around the world. Founded in the late 1800's in the United States it currently had over 700 lawyers in Asia, the Near East, Europe, and North and South America. The company's original clients included major railroads, industrial companies, and financial institutions. By the end of the 20th century, Burns-Devon had expanded its client breadth to represent a large range of international business activities and clients in multiple jurisdictions ranging from e-commerce and high technology to the large multinational conglomerates in the rail, automotive and banking sectors.

3. Reprinting. When substantial quotations are used from published sources, permission to reprint must be secured from the publisher. Substantial means any quote longer than 50 words. The exact indication of the source, including title of the report, article or book, as well as the author, publisher, date of publication and page number, must accompany each quotation.

4. Abbreviations. An appropriate abbreviation can follow the first usage of a name in the body of the case. For example, Theatre New Brunswick can become (TNB) for the rest of the case, statistical process control can become (SPC), and internal rate of return can become (IRR).

5. Putting Assignment Questions in the Case. It is not normal to include assignment questions at the beginning or end of a case. Such a practice can severely limit the use of the case, since other instructors may wish to use it for an entirely different purpose than that implied by the questions. The conventional practice is for each instructor who uses the case to develop his or her own assignment questions separately from the case. Any assignment questions or special instructions should become a part of the teaching note.

An Example

To illustrate the editing task using some of the case editing suggestions described above, consider the title, opening and concluding paragraphs of a newly written case now at the editing stage, as shown in Exhibit 7-2.

Applying some of the C words from the case editing checklist to the paragraphs in Exhibit 7-2, the need for corrections is evident.

Exhibit 7-2
OPENING AND ENDING PARAGRAPHS OF A NEWLY WRITTEN CASE

THE CASE OF THE EMBEZZLED FUNDS

Molly O'Neil, Vice-President of Human Resources at Dynamic Investments Ltd., picks up the ringing telephone on Monday morning, January 17, 2000.

"Hello this is Molly O'Neil speaking."

"Molly Joe Carter from the Chronicle. What are you going to do about the funds embezzlement scam reported by one of your employees in today's paper?"

"Joe I just saw the article myself not ten minutes ago. I am very concerned, I will check it out and get back to you as soon as I can."

Molly hung up the phone in a troubled mood. "What a way to start a Monday morning," she ponders.

-
-
-

Conclusion

Mollie Neil had spent all day Monday and Tuesday snarfing around the tent of the embezzlement scam. She was now ready to fulfill her mandate to the President.

Consistency

The opening paragraphs are not consistent with the conclusion. In the opening paragraphs the story line cut is made after Molly hangs up the phone and the decision frame cut is to call Joe back with the results of her investigation as soon as possible. In the conclusion, the story line cut has moved forward to the end of Tuesday and the decision frame cut has Molly ready to fulfill a request from the President but with no stated time frame. The case writer needs to reconsider the most appropriate story line and decision frame cuts.

Correctness

These paragraphs are incorrect in several ways. First, in the opening paragraphs the word "picks" must be changed to "picked" and "ponders" changed to "pondered." Second, there are spelling errors. Is the decision maker's name "Molly" or "Mollie?" Is it "O'Neil" or "Neil? " Third, in the quotes, there should be commas after the words "Hello," "Molly" and "Joe,", a period after the word "concerned," as well as a closed quotation mark after the word "can."

Clarity

In the conclusion, "snarfing around the tent of the embezzlement scams" is a colorful phrase but not easily understood. A better statement would be, "talking to people and gathering information about the alleged embezzlement scam." Furthermore, the last sentence could be changed to, "She was now ready to respond to Joe."

Case Title

"The Case of the Embezzled Funds" is a case title that is too evaluative and conclusive. More appropriate case titles could be Dynamic Investments Ltd. or Molly O'Neil.

Given the full text of the Molly O'Neil case, each of the C words should be applied in editing the case.

Once the edited case is acceptable to the supervisor and to the case writer, if different from the supervisor, external approval to use the case must be obtained from the source organization. The necessary steps in securing release are discussed in the next chapter.

CHAPTER EIGHT

release

Obtaining formal permission from the contributing organization to use the case for educational purposes is the vital conclusion to the second phase of the case writing process. A case writer must secure an official release from the organization before publishing or using the case. This chapter presents the purposes of release, the required tasks for obtaining the release and the various kinds of releases.

RELEASE PURPOSES

Release is one key distinguishing characteristic of case and serves four important purposes:

1. Release Assures Academic Honesty

Release is a guarantee that the case writer has truly gone to the field and researched and documented a real situation involving real people facing real issues. It distinguishes the case from fiction or from one generated from generalized experience.

2. Release Authenticates the Data

Release verifies that the information presented in the case is accurate and fairly reflects the facts available and opinions expressed at the time the issue was addressed in the organization. It is not unusual for cases to be disguised at the request of the participating organization. Some case information may have been changed to assure confidentiality but every effort has been taken to make certain the story line and the issues have been properly preserved. Release means instructors do not have to apologize for or justify the case information in the face of student argumentation or disagreement with the information as presented. It is quite acceptable for instructors to say, "That's the way it was for this company and let's use their facts and data to assist our discussion of the analyses and possible decisions."

3. Release Grants Permission to Use the Case

Release grants permission to use the case for educational purposes. In addition, release provides the legal basis for adding the disclaimer and copyright statement to the title page of the case. Copyright means ownership, and no person, except the case author, can change anything in the case or in the way the material is presented.

4. Release Maintains Positive Relations

Release helps to develop and maintain positive relations between the academic institution and the contributing organization. Because cases do not last forever, case writers have to keep going back to the field looking for new cases. Even if future new cases are never written in the same organization, maintaining good relations is a desirable outcome. The academic says, "I would like to use your case." The practitioner says, "I like what you have written." Obtaining a release is a win-win outcome.

TASKS FOR OBTAINING RELEASE

There are four tasks for obtaining final release following the preparation of the edited case and before using the case in class.

Release Request

Once the edited case is complete, the case writer assembles a package of materials. This package includes copies of the case, the release form (see Exhibit 8-1) and a covering letter (see Exhibit 8-2). If this package is faxed or e-mailed to the contact person, the case writer should provide clear instructions on how to make and communicate any corrections. If this package is delivered by post-mail, the case writer should include a second copy of the case and a self-addressed stamped envelope. Mailing two copies of the case allows the contact person to make whatever corrections are deemed necessary on one copy to be returned while retaining the second copy. The covering letter provides an opportunity to thank the contact person for the cooperation received and to instruct the contact on his or her tasks associated with the release.

It is common practice for the case writer to fill in the title of the case, the position of the contact person and the contributing organization's address before sending the release form. The contact person can then just check off the appropriate boxes on the release form and sign on the signature line. The objective of this task is to make it easy for the contact person to review the case and return the signed release form along with any necessary corrections as quickly as possible.

The preliminary teaching note is not shared with the contact person and so does not have to be released. This note is the property of the case writer and should be carefully protected.

Exhibit 8-1
SAMPLE RELEASE FORM

Date:_____

We have read the case entitled _____
and we hereby authorize the use of this material:

- ☐ By the University

- ☐ By other Schools with which the University operates a case exchange program

- ☐ By other organizations requesting this material for use in educational or training programs only

- ☐ In printed casebook/textbooks

- ☐ In electronic formats

This case is released: ☐ without change

   ☐ with corrections as indicated

Signature _____

Position _____

Company _____

If corrections are indicated, a copy of the final released version will be returned to you.

Exhibit 8-2
SAMPLE COVER LETTER

Date

Company/Organization Address

Dear _____:

Please find enclosed two copies of the_____
_____ case. I hope you will be able to release it as we provisionally agreed.

I have tried my best to use the data provided to write a case which will contribute to the education of our students. If in reading the case you should find certain errors or wish to suggest certain additions or deletions, I would appreciate your pointing these out to me. Please mark them on the extra copy of the case and return this corrected copy. Also, please sign the enclosed release form and return it at your earliest convenience.

Thank you very much for your kind cooperation and assistance.

Yours sincerely,

Name   _____

Title   _____

Address   _____

Enclosures: Two copies of the case
             Release form
             Self-addressed envelope

Follow-up

The case writer may have to expedite the release as per the time plan (see Chapter 5) with the contact person. Receiving a case, reviewing it and signing the release does not have as high a priority for the contact person as it does for the case writer. Therefore, the case writer may sometimes need to make a follow-up phone call, or send a fax or e-mail message to the case contact to expedite the process.

Correcting and Filing

Upon receiving the signed release form, the case writer makes the necessary changes, additions and deletions and returns a copy of the corrected case to the contact person along with a letter of thanks for the release and the suggested improvements to the case. It is also good practice for the case writer to return any confidential company documents, reports and materials that may have been provided during the data collection process.

For many case writers, the correcting and filing task completes Phase 2 of the case writing process. The release form is filed with the case, and the case can now be used for educational purposes.

For case writers at the Ivey Business School and at other schools which maintain a bibliography of case titles, as well as those case writers who want to submit their case(s) to other case distribution centers (see Appendix 3), such as the European Case Clearing House (ECCH), there is one more required task. This task will ultimately be necessary for any institution wishing to produce its own bibliography of cases.

Registration

Case writers who submit their cases to a case distribution center for registration are required to complete a case information form (see Exhibit 8-3 for a sample). This form provides a concise summary of the characteristics of the case to

Exhibit 8-3
SAMPLE CASE INFORMATION FORM

CASE TITLE: **CASE NUMBER:**

ELECTRONIC FILE NAME: **NUMBER OF PAGES:**
Software used:

AUTHOR(s): Prepared by:
              Under the direction of:

Release attached: ☐   **Restricted release:** ☐ Yes ☐ No

Teaching note available: ☐ Yes ☐ No

TEACHING AREA: (check one)
Accounting	☐	Information Systems	☐
Business Policy/Strategy	☐	International Business	☐
Communications	☐	Management Science	☐
Economics &		Marketing	☐
Environmental Change	☐	Operations	☐
Entrepreneurship	☐	Organizational Behavior	☐
Finance	☐	Other	☐

This material is written for student analysis at the following level(s):
Executive Education ☐   Graduate ☐   Undergraduate ☐
Pre-university ☐

ABSTRACT:

KEY ISSUES OR CONCEPTS INVOLVED:
1.   3.   5.
2.   4.   6.

DECISION MAKER: Male ☐   Female ☐   Position:

SETTING OF CASE:
Department: (accounting, marketing, etc.)
Geographic: (province/state/country)
Industry:
Company/Organization Size: ☐ Small ☐ Medium ☐ Large
Year of Case:

AUTHOR(S) SIGNATURE(S):   **DATE:**

let other case users know what the case is all about. Ivey Publishing and Harvard Business School Publishing, for example, put information from these forms on their web sites. ECCH has a system called Case On Line Information System (COLIS). Case users can find out what is available in these case bibliographies using key words to search among the case information forms. Appendix 4 lists some of the major case distribution centers of the world. At the time of registration, the case distribution center assigns a code number to the case.

KINDS OF RELEASE

Implied throughout this book has been the traditional kind of release. There are other kinds. But first a few more words on traditional release.

Traditional Release

A traditional release, by far the most common kind of release, allows unrestricted use of the case for educational purposes by the copyright holder. The copyright holder, in turn, can grant others the right to use the case.

Restricted Release

A restricted release limits case use to the author only, to a particular course, to a particular institution or to a particular publication. It is not available for use in other publications or by unauthorized others. Sometimes contributing organizations want to prevent a wider use of the case for their own reasons.

Multiple Release

Sometimes a case requires a release by more than one party. Hence, two or more release forms accompany a single case. Some examples where multiple release may be required are those cases involving a union-management issue where both parties need to sign off. Other examples may include public policy cases involving conflicting interest groups, or professional practice firms where release may be necessary both from the client and from the service provider.

Delayed Release

With a delayed release, the contact person releases the case with the proviso that the case is not to be used before a future date. Occasionally, a case contains sensitive and current data, and the contributing organization requests a moratorium on using the case until a specified amount of time has passed.

Re-release

Sometimes a case just does not work very well in its initial class test and changes in the case information would make the case a better teaching vehicle. When the author makes substantive changes to the case, it is necessary to request a re-release. When the changes to a case by the case author are cosmetic in nature, re-release is not necessary.

Release Not Required

Cases written from the public record do not require a release. In the interest of maintaining positive relations with the practitioner community, it is good professional practice for the case writer to send such a case to the organization about which the case is written. Even though formal release is not required, asking whether or not the facts are truthfully stated shows respect.

A case writer who has carefully and professionally executed each step in the first two phases of the case writing process can expect release to follow without difficulty. A "win-win" outcome pleases all parties. If a case writer is not careful and professional throughout the whole process, then the risk of non-release increases. Non-release means high losses in time, energy and money, resulting in frustration and dissatisfaction for those involved.

Once the final release has been obtained and the changes, if any, requested by the participating organization have been made in the final version of the case, only then can the case be considered ready for the next step, the class test.

CHAPTER NINE

teaching note and class test

Every case should be class tested after it has been released, to determine if it meets the educational objectives and if further changes would make it a better case. Before the class test, however, the teaching note needs to be completed. This chapter, therefore, covers the preparation of the teaching note first, followed by the class test and further case alterations and re-release.

THE TEACHING NOTE

Before the released case can be tested in class, the person instructing the class needs to prepare a teaching or instructor's note. Fortunately, a good start for this document was made after the rough drafting of the case. The preliminary teaching note's primary purpose was to check the quality of the information provided in the rough draft. The purpose of the complete teaching note is to help the instructor prepare for class. Typical teaching note headings are provided in Exhibit 9-1. Seven of these 14 headings have already been addressed during the preliminary teaching note discussion in Chapter 7. As part of his or her teaching note preparation, the instructor should review the immediate and basic issues, the teaching objectives, the suggested student assignment and the case analysis (answers to the suggested student assignment questions). During this review the instructor should check for completeness and congruence between the final case and the preliminary teaching note. This is not a minimal task, especially if significant additions, deletions or other changes have been made after the rough draft.

Exhibit 9-1
TEACHING NOTE HEADINGS

1. Case Title
2. Brief Synopsis of the Case
3. Immediate Issue(s) *(the case decision maker's key concerns)*
4. Basic Issue(s) *(the instructor's reasons for using the case in the course)*
5. Teaching Objectives
6. Suggested Student Assignment
7. Suggested Additional Reading/Data Gathering
8. Possible Teaching Aids *(such as samples, advertising material, photos, articles, videos, computer programs, CD ROMs, visitors to class)*
9. Discussion Questions for Use in Class *(to use if the discussion dies or to raise issues if not covered)*
10. Case Analysis *(the answers to the suggested student assignment questions)*
11. Additional Points to Raise *(beyond the student assignment questions)*
12. Suggested Time Plan *(how total class time might be divided)*
13. Teaching Suggestions
14. Case Teaching Plan *(the instructor's supplement to the Case Preparation Chart)*

The additional headings of the teaching note not covered in the preliminary stage are briefly explained here. A more complete coverage of preparing for a case class can be found in Chapter 4 of *Teaching with Cases*.

Suggested Additional Reading/Data Gathering

The instructor may wish to assign additional readings from texts, journals or other sources or additional data gathering from a variety of sources, including the Internet. In this section of the teaching note, a variety of such references may be listed. Clearly, this section will require updating or changes over time and will vary with different uses of the cases in courses other than the one for which the case was originally written.

Possible Teaching Aids

There may be a variety of ways in which the learning of participants can be enhanced. Teaching aids may include: annual reports, company brochures or pamphlets, web site information, product samples, advertising material, photos, articles, videos, computer programs, CD ROMs and visitors to class.

Discussion Questions for Use in Class

Foreseeing the possibility that the class discussion may require some stimulation at certain points or that some key issues have not been raised by class participants, the instructor may wish to prepare beforehand a set of useful questions pertaining to this case. These questions may not have to be used, but are available, if needed.

Additional Points to Raise

Different from potential discussion questions, additional points to raise cover topics outside the standard assignment questions. These points may include events prior to the story line in the case or afterwards, as well as relevant other events in the industry or in the world.

Teaching Suggestions

Teaching suggestions cover a wide range of potential topics. They could be: "Be sure to cover the additional readings before starting the case discussion" and "Avoid calling early on someone with experience in this industry" or "The calculations required will challenge most students, and it is necessary to set a significant amount of time aside for the quantitative analysis" or "For undergraduates, it is best to review the immediate and basic issues first, while graduate students can start directly with alternatives." Other teaching suggestions could be: "Starting with a vote on the two alternatives works well" or "Identifying all possible alternatives before discussing any specific one is useful."

The Case Teaching Plan

The Case Teaching Plan (See Exhibit 9-2) is extensively discussed in *Teaching with Cases,* Chapter 4. It covers the agenda, the time plan, the participation plan and the board plan.

The agenda lists the various topic options for a class as shown in Exhibit 9-2.

The time plan allocates total class time to the selected topic areas in the agenda. Not every agenda item is covered in every class.

The participation plan identifies whether the instructor intends to call on specific class participants for different agenda items or to invite/wait for volunteers.

The preference list identifies individuals who are not on the call list, but who will receive preference if they volunteer at the same time as other volunteers.

EXHIBIT 9-2
CASE TEACHING PLAN

Case Title: Course/Program: Date:

Time   Agenda   **Participants**

___   1. Introduction

Preference Participant List	
1.	5.
2.	6.
3.	7.
4.	8.

___   2. Next/Other Classes

___   3. Comments, Questions

                                     Volunteer (V) / Call List

___   4. Reading Discussion   V   or _____

___   5. Case Introduction   V   or _____

___   6. Teaching Aids

        7. Assignment Questions

___   1 _____   V   or _____
___   2 _____   V   or _____
___   3 _____   V   or _____
___   4 _____   V   or _____

___   8. Conclusion
___   Total

Board Plan

Issues	Analysis	Decision Criteria
Analysis	Alternatives	Action/Implementation
		Missing Info/Assumptions

© 2001, Richard Ivey School of Business

The board plan shows the preferred location for major topic areas, if the instructor uses a board during the class discussion session to record points made by participants. "What would I want the board to look like at the end of the class?" is the question guiding the board plan. The board plan included in the Case Teaching Plan (Exhibit 9-2) is based on the major steps in the standard problem solving model and represents one reasonable way of organizing material on a board.

Please note that the Case Teaching Plan varies with each teaching of the case and has to be prepared anew. Other parts of the teaching note may vary less with time.

Once the instructor has prepared a satisfactory teaching note, he or she can commence the class test. Obviously, after the class test, the "guesses" in this first attempt at a teaching note can be assessed, and significant changes to the next draft of the teaching note may result.

CLASS TEST

A newly written case is not complete until it has been class tested at least once, and the final corrections to the case have been made. Technically, every time an instructor teaches a case she or he has not taught before, this teacher is class testing the case. However, in the case writing context a class test is the first time a newly written case is used with a student group and the subsequent time that a revised or re-released version of the same case is tried again. If the educator is the author of the case or the supervisor of a research associate who wrote the case, she or he can make the necessary revisions after teaching the case. If the case is taught by someone else, that teacher does not have the right to make any changes.

The Need for Class Testing

No matter how carefully a case has been crafted, it is always possible that it could be improved if further changes were made. There is a mistaken perception that once the case is released it is finished. Just because the contributing organization agrees to the correctness of the case data and gives permission for others to use the case does not mean the case is perfect.

Once the revisions the contributing organization has requested have been incorporated, the case now represents the best effort of the case writer and his or her company contacts. Therefore, it should be close to being right. However, student eyes have not yet seen the case. And students have not patiently labored over every sentence and detail. Yet, they are the customers. If, in the time that students have available for individual preparation and small group discussion they found the case not to their taste, not clear, too long, imprecise, missing data, difficult to read, ambiguous or unappetizing, then the case may have to be revised. Unfortunately, there are far too many 95 percent cases in the system where even 15 minutes of additional work by the case author(s) could have made a vast improvement to the usefulness, clarity, completeness and enjoyment of the case.

It is unfortunate that the release has to come before the class test, because one of the stumbling blocks to revisions after release is the fear of the need for re-release. There is angst associated with the admission, "I told you at the time of release the case was great, but now it needs some change." Release is a prerequisite for class testing. The case writer should make it clear to the company contact that further change(s) based on the class test are likely to be forthcoming.

Kinds of Class Test

There are several ways in which a case can be class tested. The common one is when the educator involved in creating the case teaches it. A variation on this theme is when a colleague teaches it and the case writer may or may not attend the test.

Popular options in case schools are to use a new case first as an exam, report, student presentation or case competition. These options have two benefits. In the first place, no chance exists that one or more students have had exposure to this case in other classes, courses or programs. Secondly, in these settings the students will prepare carefully, assuring that the case will be read, analyzed and agonized over. If the educational objectives are not met or information is wrongly perceived, it will be evident from the exams and reports submitted. If a class is taught subsequently with the same students and the same case, the quality of the feedback on the case is likely to be good.

If the case is taught in a normal class setting, it is a good idea for the instructor to let the students know that this is the first time the case has ever been taught and to enlist their feedback. "I would really appreciate your looking for any errors, clarifications or anything that would help make this case better." Our experience is that a small percentage of the class takes this seriously and gives wonderful feedback, ranging from grammatical errors and factual inconsistencies to insightful suggestions as to how their task of reading and preparing the case could be improved if certain changes were made.

Some instructors believe inviting the key person in the case to attend the class test adds reality and excitement to the occasion. Other instructors believe this is the worst time to invite the focal person in the case (see *Teaching with Cases*, Chapter 8).

What Needs Testing?

There are two main questions to address in a class test:

1. Does the new case meet its educational objectives?
2. Is the quality of the presentation of the new case satisfactory?

1. Does the new case meet its educational objectives?

Clearly, this is the first and foremost question to be addressed. However, a slight rephrasing might highlight the purpose of the class test, "Would further changes to the new case improve the achievement of the educational objectives?" The follow-up questions then become, "What changes need to be made to give better results, and is it reasonable to make such changes? Would the inclusion or deletion of certain information in the case make it a better teaching vehicle?" Please notice that one option that does not exist is the falsification of case data to make it more dramatic or interesting. It is not permissible to have the president say, "I am quitting tomorrow if you don't go along with my plans," or change a $5,000 machine into a $500,000 machine when, in reality, these facts are not true.

For the moment, assuming that the case itself might be improvable with respect to its educational objectives, typical signals, using the Case Difficulty Cube dimensions, could be:

The students have difficulty:

1. performing the necessary analytical work to deal with the decision or problem resolution part of the case;
2. connecting the appropriate concepts, theories and frameworks to the main case issue(s);
3. organizing, sorting, combining the information available, specifying missing information or making reasonable assumptions.

Additional signals are class apathy, a number of students coming up after class saying, "I don't know what that case was all about" or "Am I right that this is what you were trying to achieve with this case?"

2. Is the quality of the presentation of the case satisfactory?

The presentation quality of the case may also impact its ability to meet educational objectives. Prime concerns here deal with the ability of the students to understand the case data correctly. Is the organization of the case as good as it could be? Would additional subtitles help? Would a few additional sentences help make an idea clearer? Would it be helpful to add an exhibit showing the product, the process flow, the organization chart, the memo, the key excerpts from a letter, the report or proposal, the map, the machine, the plant layout, the chart, the advertisement?

Would it be helpful if we changed the wording, showed all figures in a consistent way, summed the figures in the columns, deleted a meaningless paragraph, added dates to various events?

It is assumed here that all spelling and grammatical errors that still show up at this stage will automatically be corrected. Occasionally, such gremlins do persist and create a bad impression.

The prime judge of whether the case can be improved for educational objectives is the teacher. Since many factors can contribute to a poor class case reception during the class test, the conclusion that it is the fault of the case itself needs to be examined carefully. The section below on interpreting test results identifies a host of non-case issues which could contribute to a poor class test.

Interpreting Class Test Results

It is possible and absolutely wonderful that a new case is enthusiastically received during the class test and that not a critical word is heard. Those instructors who have experienced such euphoria also know that it does not happen all the time. It is more common that the class did not go as well as hoped. Now the detective work starts to find out why.

Blaming the case may be psychologically satisfying but it may or may not be the right thing to do. Exhibit 9-3 presents a cause and effect diagram identifying potential contributors to an unsatisfactory case class experience. The important conclusion is that many factors contribute to a case class result and the case itself is only one factor. Some obvious other factors include (1) the assignment, (2) the degree of preparedness by the students and (3) the way the class was taught.

1. The assignment. Normally, the assignment used in the class test of the case comes from the preliminary and full teaching notes. At the time the case was written, certain assumptions about the placement of the case in the course, the theory covered to date or the time of the year may have been made which are no longer valid. Perhaps asking the students first to draw a process flow diagram, an organization chart, do a ratio analysis, examine the profitability of a product line, or do a consumer analysis might have made the other questions in the case easier. Perhaps asking them to come up with at least three alternatives is better than asking them what action they would take and why. The point here is that the assignment, particularly for students new to the case method, can make a substantial difference in the way students prepare and participate.

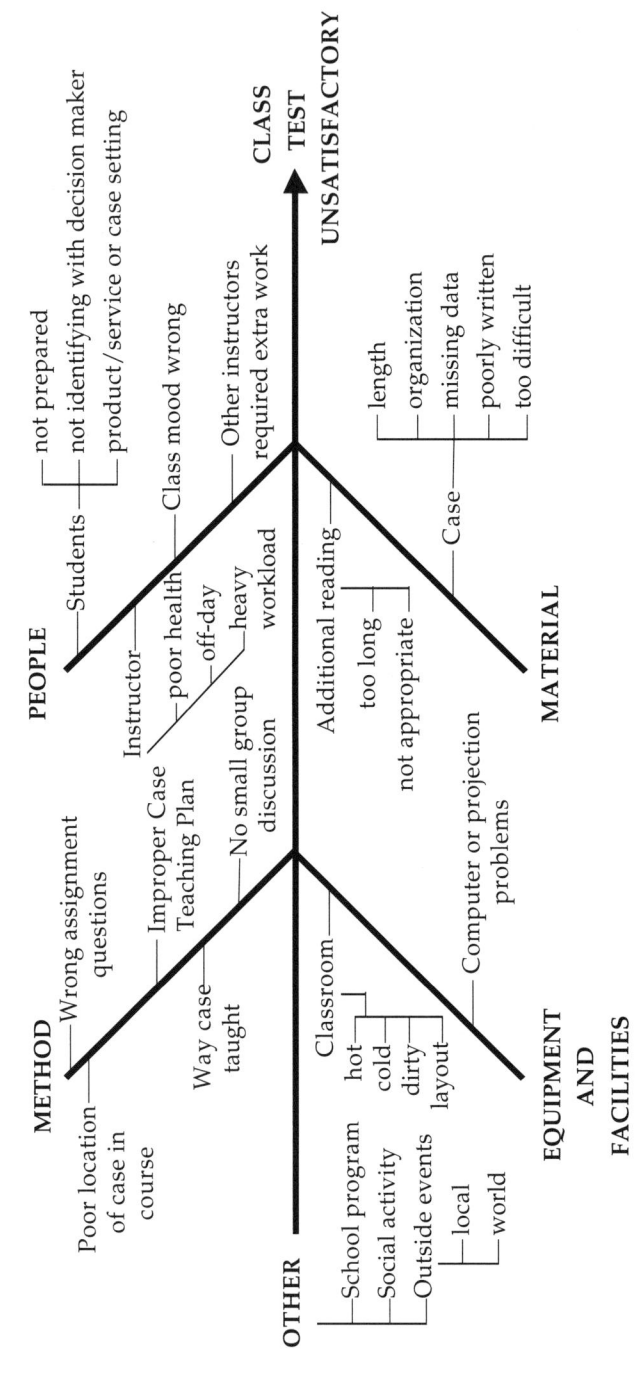

Exhibit 9-3
CASE CLASS TEST CAUSE AND EFFECT DIAGRAM

2. The degree of preparedness of the students. Obviously, if a class is not properly prepared, the class test of a case becomes meaningless. Thus, if students fumble about, have difficulty dealing with case facts, are reluctant to talk and act evasively, it may have nothing to do with the case, but everything with last night's party or the exam in another course.

3. The way the case was taught. Instructors need to explore to find the best way to teach a case and it may not always be obvious. Clearly, experience helps, but even experienced case teachers may not find the best way to teach a case the first time around. Some instructors believe it takes at least three iterations to develop the correct teaching approach. Thus, after the class test the standard question should be, "Could I have taught this case better and how?"

In one executive program, we had a case dealing with a consultant's report that was full of interesting issues, or so we thought. Yet, in its first three class tests, it failed to generate the kind of excitement we believed it should. Only at the fourth try were we able to get the timing in the course, the assignment and the way it was taught right. Had we not been so convinced that the case itself was a good one, we would have discarded it after the second try.

CASE REVISIONS AND RE-RELEASE

It is important to make case revisions quickly after the class test. Language, grammatical changes and data deletions do not require a re-release, but it is good practice to send the improved version of the case to the contributing organization. It is a good opportunity to share the results of the class test and to let the contact person know he or she has not been forgotten.

If additional data are included and substantive changes are made to the case, re-release becomes mandatory. It is thoughtful to underline or highlight the changes made so that the case contact does not have to re-read the whole case to find out what changes are requested. The explanation that, because of the class test, further improvements to the case will make it a better one for both students and teachers, is an excellent argument for granting re-release. Failure to request a re-release may result in hard feelings and even the withdrawal of the original release. Good corporate relations and ethical case writing require that this step, also, be included in the case writing process when necessary.

Teachers Who Are Not Authors That Wish to Make Changes to Cases

It is common that well-written cases are used by a variety of teachers in a variety of courses in a variety of circumstances. It would be a miracle if each of these teachers was equally satisfied with the content and presentation of the original case. The urge, therefore, to modify the case, to insert or delete data, or to fabricate a few different twists to make this case more suitable, can be overwhelming. Case writing ethics do not permit such changes. Only the author(s) and the institution(s) holding the copyright can grant permission to make any changes to the original case.

A teacher who wishes to use a case for a different purpose can change the assignment. If a teacher does not like the date or the country setting of the case, he or she can say in the assignment, "If this case setting was in our country, in this year, how would it affect your analysis and recommendations?"

If a teacher does not like the decision maker chosen as the focal person in the case, he or she can assign, "If you were in the position of the President or ... instead of the Sales Manager, how would it change your answers to the above questions?"

If a teacher does not like the figures used in the case, he or she can ask, "What if this organization was not profitable? If this machine cost three times as much? If the labor costs were X% higher or Y% lower? If the hurdle rate was …?"

No permission needs to be sought from any copyright holder to ask any assignment questions.

Generally speaking, the worse the reception the first time the case is class tested, the greater the need for more tests. One cannot assume that the first fix-up of the case will be sufficient. There is a matter of personal taste in cases. Some cases are popular just as some music and films are popular, others are not. Instructors can fan such popularity with their own enthusiasm in the class. It confers high status to go into a class with one's own case. It sends a message to students, "I care enough about you and this course to develop my own material. I was able to persuade a real-life manager to provide this case. I am also willing to involve you in this whole process and run the risk of your disapproval."

The teaching note and class test, further improvements to the case and re-release (if required) complete Phase 3 of the case writing process. There are, however, a number of issues surrounding the case writing process which will be addressed in the final chapter.

CHAPTER TEN

other considerations

A variety of topics pertaining to case writing still need to be addressed. These include: case length, case life and updating old cases, case writing and consulting, academic credit for case writing, using others to write cases, case costs and financing and other forms of cases.

CASE LENGTH

The question of case length in terms of how much data to include has already been addressed in Chapter 7. However, in terms of current trends in simulating business reality and processing the data for an educational learning experience, case length is an ongoing issue. On the presentation dimension of the Case Difficulty Cube, too many cases have a difficulty level of three. In certain courses it is not unusual to assign cases of 30, 40 or even 60 pages on a regular basis, for students who have three such preparations a day. Case length, or the volume of case data provided, is always a significant concern to the students.

Some case writers think that providing more details makes cases more realistic. Some believe that business is becoming more complex and the tools more sophisticated, therefore you need more information to describe the situation adequately. Others insist that students must learn to sort out relevant from irrelevant information and that, in real life, information is not neatly organized any way. While long cases may help students learn how to sort information for relevance, instructors also have to pursue other teaching objectives. It is easier to write long cases than short ones. Long cases often reveal a lack of clear understanding of the teaching objectives as well as an insensitivity to students' time constraints. Long cases also encourage students to take shortcuts, such as preparing only every third case or dividing reading and preparation among each other.

It is our experience that participants have difficulty completing a thorough preparation for a case exceeding ten pages of text plus exhibits, assuming a normal two-hour preparation period per case and three cases a day. Students can often do little more than scan long cases. If cases are not well prepared, the following small group and large group discussions are weak. The cumulative effect of using a high proportion of long cases is that students actually end up learning less in their courses and program.

CASE LIFE AND UPDATING OLD CASES

Case Life and Turnover Rate

Cases do not last forever. One interesting interpretation of quality relates to the useful life of the case. The better the case the longer it may last! Case obsolescence was discussed in Chapter 1 under the heading "Why Write Cases?" A related question is: What rate of case turnover should be expected in a case course? Cases written for courses in some areas of management are more at risk of becoming obsolete faster than in other areas. Except for some "classic" cases where the issue they disclose and principles they invoke are ageless, a standard expectation is that between 10% and 25 % of the total number of cases will be replaced every year. The turnover rate will vary with the subject and the resources available to develop new cases in a given institution.

Cases should not be replaced just for the sake of replacement, however. This practice could lead to substituting good cases with equally good cases and thus wasting money; or worse, replacing good cases with less effective ones. The driving principle should be, "Is the old case meeting my teaching purposes? If yes, let's keep it; if not, let's replace it with a better one."

Revision and Updating

To extend the life of a case, an educator may be tempted to revise or update it. The excuse is that it takes too much time and work to write a new case to substitute for an already adequate or good vehicle. Cases can be updated in more than one way: changing dates, adjusting figures to deal with inflation, upgrading the technology and even modernizing the issue. The result may end up looking like a coat made from an old curtain.

Updating cases is not something that we endorse as a solution to keeping teaching material current. The principle of truth in representation is the key factor here. Also obtaining a re-release on a 20-year-old case may be difficult, if not impossible. The company may not even exist anymore. Revisions to a case, if absolutely necessary, should preferably be performed by its original author and always be documented at the bottom of the first page and dated. But we would much rather encourage the educator to write a new case than to tamper with an obsolete one.

CASE WRITING AND CONSULTING

It is not unusual for case writers to be asked for their opinion or to be tempted to give free advice to the contacts in the contributing organization during the case writing process. We believe that a distinct separation should be maintained between case writing and consulting activities at all times. Mixing the two can only result in conflict of interest. One cannot be an impartial observer or reporter and, at the same time, a consultant making recommendations that impact on the organization and its personnel, without affecting the information and data collection process.

Case writers should resist requests by people in contributing organizations to evaluate decisions taken or to make suggestions for future action. The best way to prevent such requests is to emphasize that the case is written strictly for educational purposes. The immediate benefits to the contributing organization are the articulation of an issue and the possible creation of in-house training materials.

If an educator gets involved in consulting in an organization and believes case writing opportunities exist, we suggest that these two sets of activities be separated by a reasonable period of time. Then there is no confusion in anyone's mind as to the purpose of the work in the organization. Moreover, it is usually preferable that the case issues be different from the consulting issues.

ACADEMIC CREDIT FOR CASE WRITING

In the academic world there are a number of questions relating to the respectability and scholarly nature of case development activities. As pressures for publications and research output mount for those who are on a promotion or tenure track, the academic worth of case writing is often questioned.

Three typical questions are: 1) Is case writing worthy of academic credit? 2) Is a case a publication? and 3) Is case writing a research or teaching materials development activity? There is certainly no unanimity on any of these three questions.

1. Is Case Writing Worthy of Academic Credit?

The three camps on the case writing worthiness of academic credit question are yes, no and maybe. It is not surprising that the prominence of case teaching in the academic institution tends to influence the answer. The more prominent the use of case teaching, the more likely case writing will be given some form of academic credit or recognition.

In institutions that do not use cases very much, case writing normally receives little or no recognition for promotion and tenure. Unfortunately, some of the most vocal opponents of recognition are those who know the least about cases and do not write cases themselves. Consequently, young faculty in these institutions have difficulty mustering the enthusiasm and resources to engage in case writing and, if they do, it is at a certain risk.

On the other hand, institutions totally committed to the case method tend to recognize case development as one of many factors to be considered in the evaluation of faculty members for promotion. The amount of credit granted may depend on a variety of considerations. For example, a case may represent a new thrust into a significant area of management; it may lead to better academic insight, and even form the basis for a new theory. The writing of such cases may receive significant recognition. Whether cases are used by other academics in the same institution or elsewhere, the number of copies used per year, and whether cases are published in texts or journals or received an award in a case competition, are additional considerations. However, the writing of a case which is a duplicate of an older one will offer little contribution in terms of conceptualization or teaching notes, and consequently may bring little credit to its author.

The two remaining questions on whether a case is a publication and whether case writing is research or course development are significant if the answer to the first question is affirmative.

2. Is a Case a Publication?

The academic worth of a case as a publication is difficult to establish compared to a refereed article in a reputable journal. Some institutions ask senior faculty members or outside experts to review the cases and teaching notes written by others. Some national and international case method associations referee cases for publication and sponsor case writing competitions. Data can be collected on the use of cases inside and outside the institution, and whether they appeared in any textbook or not. But what do you do with the cases written for an elective course taught exclusively by the case writer? Interestingly enough, student evaluations of specific cases are rarely requested and, if they are, seldom taken into account. Given the trend towards privatization of management education and the growing perception of the student as consumer, student evaluations may become more important.

As long as a case accomplishes its educational objectives, it meets the first and foremost requirement of case quality. Nevertheless, a perfectly effective short case written for an introductory course may receive a poor evaluation from referees who do not value the scholarly and unique nature of the issue, or the case research process, or the presentation of the case itself. This factor may be another reason for the unfortunate tendency to write long cases.

3. Is Case Writing a Research or Teaching Materials Development Activity?

Many academics think that cases must be viewed exclusively as teaching vehicles and, therefore, represent course development. The problem is that in many academic institutions teaching performance and teaching materials development do not get much recognition; therefore, case writing is attributed little value in promotion and tenure decisions.

Even though appropriate academic credit for case development may be difficult to come by, it is obviously desirable to have a clear understanding within an academic institution on the degree of recognition for case writing and on the evaluation criteria.

USING OTHERS TO WRITE CASES

Some educators have the opportunity to use the assistance of others to write cases. These other people may be research associates, research assistants or even students. While research associates may be experienced case writers and full-time employees in an institution, research assistants tend to be engaged for short periods rarely exceeding one year. The issues of selection, training and supervision, covered in this section, apply to both types, even though the research associate may know more about case writing than the educator he or she works with. Students rarely write more than one case and are typically not paid for it. We will discuss student case writers separately at the end of this section.

Selection

Even with the resources available to hire assistants to write cases, not everyone chooses to do so. Some educators have had bad experiences with case writers; others feel that they can write a case in the same time that it takes to supervise an assistant to do one. Many educators lack training and supervisory skills to make the best use of hired case writers.

If a research assistant or associate is employed, what should his or her qualifications be? Effective case writing requires a unique combination of skills and knowledge. Most people agree that writing ability comes first; more specifically, the ability to report facts and opinions in an objective manner. A close second is content knowledge; that is, enough familiarity with the subject matter to know the terminology, ask pertinent questions and understand the educational implications. Other important skills are also necessary such as: good interviewing skills, the ability to build trust, openness and cooperation. Moreover, the case writer must understand the ethical issues involved in case writing and have the maturity to place the long term relationship of the institution with the contributing organization before his or her own personal interest. And of course, he or she must be self-motivated and able to work independently.

Students may be good candidates for case writing and are often hired for summer jobs. However, the main challenge for students, trained to analyze situations and make recommendations, is to leave the analysis or elements of solutions out of the case. Other people may also be excellent candidates and be willing to be case writers for a longer period of time, thus developing useful expertise with the resulting increased productivity. Case writing may be an interesting occupation for former graduates who, for a number of reasons, may not wish or be able to work full time. Writing cases gives them an opportunity to work on a reasonably flexible schedule, even at home, and, at the same time, enjoy an intellectually stimulating, varied and worthwhile activity. Some institutions find it more cost effective to have full time case writers who are generalists and can write cases in a number of areas than temporary case writers attached to specific faculty members who typically quit just when they have become proficient.

Training

Most newly hired research assistants have no prior case writing experience. They need training to be productive. Just throwing the budding case writer directly into the process with little orientation can be disastrous.

Since 1968, every year in late April, a case writing workshop has been offered at the Richard Ivey School of Business for newly hired research assistants, Ph. D. candidates and faculty from inside or outside the Business School. In less than five days, each participant actually writes a short field-based case and preliminary teaching note, working through all the steps of the case writing process. Participants review one another's cases at various stages of completion, and apply the concepts and the tools described in this book.

If attending a case writing workshop is not an option, both case writer and supervisor can at least read this book to be on the same wave length.

Supervision

The quality of the relationship between the case writer and supervisor will certainly impact positively on the productivity of the case writer and reduce potential frustrations.

It is useful for the supervisor and the case writer to work together on the Case Origin Grid and the Case Shopping List before searching for leads. It is also useful if the supervisor accompanies the new case writer at the first interview with each case lead, not only to help build rapport and introduce the case writer to the main contacts in the organization, but also to help decide on the opening paragraph and assist with the rest of the Case Plan. A clearly defined Case Plan will require the educator's involvement primarily in the early stages of the process. The supervisor's approval of the Case Plan will permit the case writer to complete the remaining stages of the case writing process with minimum supervision.

One common challenge is the lack of objectivity on the part of the case writer towards his or her own work. Extensive suggestions for re-drafting can be disappointing to both case writer and supervisor. The case writer must be flexible and responsive to suggestions, and the supervisor should be tactful and constructive in offering them. Close cooperation between these two will result in better cases completed in reasonable time.

One of the biggest frustrations experienced by case writers can be the lack of attention given by the supervisor. For example, the case writer works hard to complete a draft and meet a deadline, and the draft sits for weeks on the supervisor's desk gathering dust. Or the supervisor is the one with the contacts and the leads, but he or she is too busy to make the necessary arrangements. The educator must be able to give reasonable priority to supervising the case writer or should not consider having one. Regular and timely feedback will do a lot to keep the case writer motivated.

Interruptions and delays occur during case writing. One way to deal with these problems is to keep two or three cases going simultaneously at various stages of completion. When waiting for feedback on one case from the supervisor or release on another from the contributing organization, the case writer can work on the rough draft of a third case.

It is expected that, as the new case writer gains experience, less and less time will be required from the supervisor. It may even reach a point where an experienced case writer may know more about the process than the particular faculty member he or she works with. Part of the case writer's role then becomes sharing that knowledge with this faculty member.

Students as Case Writers

Most of the examples in this text have been taken from situations where funds were available to pay for case writing. In many academic institutions this possibility does not exist, as budgets are tight. It is not surprising, therefore, that the idea of using students to assist in case writing has been tried extensively.

Various strategies have been adopted, most of them requiring the educator to get involved at one point or another in the case writing process to complete the work. One simple way is for an instructor to ask if any student has access to an interesting case situation and to discuss this with the instructor. Normally, the volunteer student will attempt a first draft, but the instructor will have to elicit the additional information and write the final case.

Another way is to allow students to write a case in place of an exam, a report or a project, and to have the student request formal approval to follow this route. This can result in five or six good cases per course offering. It is still useful for the instructor to look carefully at the Case Plan and ensure the provisional release is obtained. Often the instructor can limit involvement to final editing and release after the course is over.

Yet another way is to make case writing mandatory as part of a course. This tends to produce lots of cases, but also lots of headaches for the instructor, as not every student has a feel for how to write a case.

No matter which of the above routes is followed, substantial up-front assistance will be required for any student in terms of determining the kinds of cases that might be useful, as well as providing training in the case writing process.

CASE COSTS AND FINANCING

It is difficult to get any hard data on case costs and financing, except that everybody agrees that it is a rather expensive way of developing teaching materials. In the literature, little reference is made to this subject.

How much does a case cost? It depends. Most institutions pay their new case writer less than the average annual pay of their graduating class. Productivity is also a factor. A new case writer will not be as productive as an experienced one. At Ivey, the normal expectation for a full-time case writer is an average of 12 cases and accompanying teaching notes per year. Adding travel costs, electronic and administrative support, telephone and supplies in addition to faculty time, the cost of a new case can be substantial.

If we look at the cost of a case per time it is taught, we can see the importance of writing quality cases quickly. Where there is no insistence on accountability, productivity, efficiency and effective communication, the case research process can easily bog down and be very expensive. Considerable idle time may creep in that could easily be reduced with better planning of case development activities. Cost effectiveness can be achieved with appropriate institutional policies and procedures, in addition to proper training.

The foregoing comments do not raise the problem of where the money can be found for case writing. As the budgets for educational institutions tighten, a natural first reaction becomes the cutting of funds for case development. Unless the professors themselves are willing to fight for the maintenance of a case development program, the activity will probably be curtailed. It is best when the commitment originates from the leaders of the institution. Standard allocation rules take the pressure off yearly ad hoc decision making. For example, some courses in some institutions are entitled to have a research assistant every one or two years. In a number of schools, case development vies with other research projects for a share of the funds and human resources.

Our experience shows that where funding is limited, innovative ways can be found to write cases inexpensively. The use of electronic communication offers potential time and travel savings. Occasionally, case development is carried out simultaneously with other research or consulting projects. As we have discussed, sometimes students can write cases as part of course requirements. Companies or associations may be willing to fund case research to promote better understanding of management problems in their field. It may even be possible to sell managers on the usefulness of funding case development for internal staff development purposes.

OTHER FORMS OF CASES

International Cases

The growing awareness of globalization and the need for relevant teaching materials substantiate the demand for good international cases.

When a case writer leaves his or her home country to write a case in another country, such a case can be called an international case. Even though there is a great usefulness to writing cases in one's home country and in one's home language(s), writing international cases complements the local effort. Often, but not always, such international cases are about managing a domestic company's business unit or subsidiary in another country. Thus, Americans may wish to write about Coca Cola's attempt to secure a foreign market. The English may wish to develop a case about British Airways in Asia.

A major advantage of writing cases about international business units owned by domestic companies is the ease of establishing the lead. Someone in the home country can provide suitable contacts abroad.

It is more unusual and often more challenging for case writers to write cases in foreign countries without any domestic connection. Finding the leads and persuading managers to cooperate may be a significant challenge. The normal approach is to network with knowledgeable individuals who have a connection to one's own educational institution as well as managers in foreign countries.

Writing cases outside one's home country raises all of the standard issues of culture, language, distance, cost and familiarity with the case method. It is beyond the scope of this book to elaborate on the social and cultural norms in the various parts of the world as they pertain to case writing. There are two aspects, however, where some additional comments may be helpful.

The high cost of travel and the challenge of finding suitable contacts make it more difficult to write cases outside of one's own country. To solve cost and content concerns, case writing can be combined with other activities including: research, sabbatical leave, international teaching or personal and business travel.

Also, for academics, co-authoring a case with someone in the same discipline in an educational institution in the foreign country is an attractive alternative. That way a local expert, sensitive to local issues and norms and familiar with the local language, can simplify the case development process considerably.

Series Cases

When two or more cases are written inside the same organization and/or on the same issue, these are called series cases. Series cases normally have the same title differentiated by a capital letter in brackets to denote a sequence, e.g. — (A) — (B) —(C). Series cases have some unique advantages and disadvantages.

Series cases allow for more elaborate exploration of an issue or organization. For example, if integration across disciplines is the educational objective, a marketing (A) case can be followed by a finance (B) case and an operations (C) case. Often, because the general background of the company does not have to be repeated in series cases, more specific information can be provided in the (B) and subsequent cases.

Series cases also permit a sequence of events to be highlighted, permitting a serial treatment along a story line and/or decision frame. For example, the (A) case can describe a situation where the problem is not even identified yet. The (B) case may deal with problem definition and information gathering, the (C) case with analysis and alternative generation, and so on.

Often, a very brief (B) or (C) case can be provided in class as direct follow-up to the previous case, and allow for a new direction and focus in the discussion. For example, in the (A) case the issue may be, "What shall we offer the union in terms of a wage increase?" Then the (B) case provided in class in electronic or other form says, "We offered a three percent wage increase and the union turned it down. What do we do now?"

The great appeal for the case writer in a series case is the opportunity to increase case output with relatively little additional effort.

Research Cases

The focus in this text is on cases used for teaching purposes. Research cases have a different purpose, and therefore do not have to center on a specific decision maker. Research cases are descriptive and may include the solutions for any problems identified. The researcher also provides his or her analysis along with the research case.

These differences aside, the actual process of case writing is similar to the one recommended in this text. The use of the Case Plan, with research hypotheses substituted for teaching objectives, facilitates the precise specification of data requirements in a consistent form across different organizations to aid subsequent analysis.

Disguise requirements parallel those of teaching cases, and release for research cases is just as relevant and important. Several good texts are available on the writing and subsequent analysis of research cases and should be consulted by those whose primary interest is in research cases.

In-house Cases

Larger organizations may wish to have cases written about decisions inside their own organization to use in internal training or development programs. The case writer may be hired from outside or be a regular employee. Case leads are easily obtained by asking for suggestions from managers familiar with the training needs and the types of situations for which they wish their employees trained.

In-house cases can usually skip or minimize the general company background section of the case, resulting in shorter cases.

It is still a good idea to get release on internal cases, both for quality control and assuring cooperation from the key decision makers. Disguising the names of the key players in the case will help prevent course or program participants from contacting the principals in the case.

If academics are invited to write in-house cases, they should try to obtain permission to use these materials outside of the company. Such permission may not always be forthcoming, but is welcome if granted. Then the external use of the case will require an appropriate general background section and a separate release.

Multimedia Cases

Paper cases have become a convenient and inexpensive way of sharing a decision faced by an individual with thousands of students. And over the years, academics and students have jointly traveled down the learning curve on how to develop and use such cases effectively.

Now new technology offers exciting options as alternatives to the standard paper cases. It is useful to remind ourselves that the purpose of the case writer is to bring a decision, problem, issue, challenge or opportunity faced by a real person in a real organization into the classroom with minimal disturbance of the reality in the transmission.

Advances in computer and telecommunications technology have made it possible for a student to visit the actual workplace, see the key person in the case, peer at the computer screen in front of this person, and take over on the keyboard with access to the same data bases and information available to the key decision maker.

Complete cases on videotape have proven a popular alternative to standard paper cases. Video cases provide a host of details not normally included in the written case. Compact discs have been used successfully by a number of experimenters around the world.

The role of the case writer in developing such multimedia cases evolves into multiple roles as script writer, producer, director and camera person.

CONCLUSION

The case method has been proven to be a wonderful way of encouraging participative learning. The challenges of effective case writing, teaching and learning have not yet been fully conquered. We believe that our three texts on these subjects represent significant advances in the current state of the art.

Appendix 1
CASE WRITING INFORMATION FOR CASE CONTACTS

What Is a Case?

A case is a description of a business situation faced by someone in an organization. Cases contain relevant data about the issue available to the key person in the case, plus background information about the organization. Cases may vary in length from one to more than 40 pages, but normally range between three and 20 pages of text, and one to ten pages of exhibits.

Why Are Cases Used?

Cases are used to enable students to learn about decision making by putting themselves in the shoes of actual managers. Students analyze situations, develop alternatives, choose action and implementation plans, and communicate and defend their findings. Cases are used to test understanding of theory, to connect theory with application, and to develop theoretical insight. Cases enable students to learn by doing and teaching others.

Why Might an Organization Wish to Participate in Developing New Cases?

A case is a donation to the process of continuing improvement in management education. Your organization will increase its exposure to thousands of students who may be more responsive to your recruitment efforts. Your organization may also choose to use the case in internal training programs, and may even benefit from the questions asked by the case writer, as impartial observer during the case development process.

Confidentiality and Release

Each case requires the consent and cooperation of the organization and the individual about whom the case is written. Throughout the case writing process, case writers maintain strict confidentiality. If preferred, anonymity of the organization, individuals and data can be assured through disguise. The case is submitted to the organization to verify the accuracy of the case content. When satisfied, a designated person in the organization signs a release form permitting the school to use the case.

Appendix 1 (continued)

Case Writer Responsibility	Time	Normal Steps	Time	Contact Person Responsibility
determines case needs		Case Origin		
requests interview	5 - 15 mins	Case Lead	5 - 15 mins	suggests date, time and place
conducts interview	1 - 2 hrs	First Interview	1 - 2 hrs	discuss current or recent issues
prepares Case Plan	2 hrs- 1 day	Case Plan Preparation		
presents Case Plan and seeks provisional release	.5 - 1 hr	Second Interview Provisional Release	.5 - 1 hr	reviews Case Plan and gives provisional release
conducts interview(s) and collects data	1 - 3 days	Data Collection	1 - 3 hrs	provides relevant data or access to others
writes rough draft and preliminary teaching note	1 day to 2 wks	Rough Draft		
edits case	2 hrs- 1 day	Edited Case		
sends case and release form		Release	.5 - 2 hrs	reviews case and signs release
makes changes and sends case	10-60 mins			receives case
class tests case, makes corrections, may request re-release	1 - 3 hrs	Class Test	15 mins	receives revised case grants re-release

Appendix 2

Appendix 2
SAMPLE CASE

Richard Ivey School of Business
The University of Western Ontario

IVEY

CASE WRITING WORKSHOP

CORAL DRUGS

Shirley Black glanced at her watch. It was 1 p.m. on January 25, 2001 and only two hours remained before her meeting about Coral Dandruff Shampoo with the vice president of purchasing. As merchandise group coordinator at Coral's head office in Columbus, Ohio, Shirley was trying to decide whether to recommend switching from a large shampoo manufacturer to a small local supplier.

CORAL DRUGS

Coral Drugs was founded in 1962. Since that time, the company had steadily expanded its chain of retail drug stores throughout the state. Currently, Coral operated 114 stores and planned to add an additional 8 to 10 stores over the next five years. Coral's retail outlets sold both prescribed and over-the-counter pharmaceutical products as well as other drug store items. This private company's strategy was focused on the further expansion of its successful retail operations. Coral had a strong financial position and intended to pursue any opportunity that had potential to increase its bottom line and was related to its retail operations.

CORAL PRIVATE-LABEL PRODUCTS

One such opportunity was the development of Coral private-label products. Since 1980, the company had aggressively developed a line of products carrying the Coral name. Currently, Coral stocked over 200 different private-

---

This case was written by Glen Luinenberg at the Case Writing Workshop under the supervision of Professors James A. Erskine and Michiel R. Leenders. It was prepared solely to provide material for class discussion. The authors do not intend to illustrate either effective or ineffective handling of a managerial situation. The authors may have disguised certain names and other identifying information to protect confidentiality.

Ivey Management Services prohibits any form of reproduction, storage or transmittal without its written permission. This material is not covered under authorization from CanCopy or any reproduction rights organization. To order copies or request permission to reproduce materials, contact Ivey Publishing, Ivey Management Services, c/o Richard Ivey School of Business, The University of Western Ontario, London, Ontario, Canada, N6A 3K7; phone (519) 661-3208; fax (519) 661-3882; e-mail cases@ivey.uwo.ca.

Copyright © 2001, Ivey Management Services Version 2001-01-18

label products. Coral was proud of its ability to bring a product to its shelves that was comparable in quality to the national brands, but offered at least a 25 percent price savings to the consumer. The company was able to sell at a better price than the national brands because it was buying directly from the manufacturer and its advertising expenditures were significantly lower. Examples of successful products included Coral Acetaminophen Tablets and Coral Vitamin Supplements.

Coral private-label products were attractive to the company for several reasons. First, the margin on these products averaged 40 percent as compared with 25 percent on national brands. Also, the product line was virtually hassle-free. Apart from the initial supplier approval, the sourcing agreement left the manufacturer responsible for all aspects of product development and investment. Consequently, Coral intended to pursue any growth opportunities this private labeling offered in the future.

SOURCE SELECTION FOR PRIVATE-LABEL PRODUCTS

Coral private-label products were purchased from 26 different suppliers. Several sourcing agreements were in contract form, while others were simply an understanding between Coral and the manufacturer. The process for developing a sourcing agreement began with an internally generated idea for a potential private-label product. Once the product idea was approved, Coral announced that it was accepting bids from manufacturing operations that wanted to produce the product. Coral carefully analyzed the potential suppliers to ensure that they were able to provide a consistent product that was comparable in quality to the leading national brands and at a price that would provide satisfactory margins. When the bid was accepted, Coral and the manufacturing company worked together to develop the final product.

Sourcing agreements left the manufacturer responsible for almost all aspects of product development. Based on specifications provided by Coral, these manufacturers generated the artwork for the product, designed the packaging, invested in any necessary equipment, and performed quality assurance. Once the product received final approval from Coral, the company simply placed an order for the product when stock was required. The order was then delivered FOB to Coral's central warehouse and shipped from there to the retail stores. Consequently, this high level of supplier autonomy made annual reevaluation of the sourcing arrangements necessary.

Appendix 2   177

SWITCHING THE SOURCING AGREEMENT FOR CORAL DANDRUFF SHAMPOO

In December, 2000, Shirley had reviewed the performance of the company that produced Coral Dandruff Shampoo, Twinney Inc.. After several requests from Coral to improve delivery terms, Twinney had indicated that it would not alter the terms originally agreed upon. Many of Coral's concerns were directly related to the location of Twinney's manufacturing plant 600 miles to the east. Consequently, in early January, Coral announced that it was accepting bids on the future production of the product. A product specification document was sent to manufacturers that were known to have the capability to produce similar products. Twinney was notified prior to the announcement and was asked to submit a bid along with the others.

TWINNEY INCORPORATED

Under the current sourcing agreement, Coral had to order full skids when purchasing its private-label dandruff shampoo from Twinney. Each skid held 4,000 units. Although the shampoo was considered an excellent product, volumes for the regular, fragranced, and trial-sized products averaged only about 20,000 units each annually. Shirley knew that the inventory carrying cost at Coral was around 2 percent a month, and felt that the company had too much money tied up in such a low-volume product. Furthermore, the three-to four-week lead time required when placing an order had been causing problems. On several occasions, the Coral central warehouse had been stocked out of the products while waiting for a skid to arrive.

Shirley could not understand why a large company like Twinney would be so unwilling to accommodate Coral's requests for improved shipping terms. Although there had never been any problems with the consistency or quality of the shampoo Coral received, Shirley Black felt that perhaps more beneficial terms could be offered by a manufacturer located closer to Coral's warehouse. It happened that Twinney's injection mold for the product had just broken down and the artwork was due for revision soon. The Twinney sourcing agreement was not in contract form and, therefore, Shirley Black believed Coral was not legally obligated to continue purchasing from Twinney.

GORMAN AND IRIZAWA LTD

Out of the many bids received, the most attractive terms were offered by a young local company, Gorman and Irizawa Ltd. (G & I). The bidder agreed to similar responsibilities as those in the existing Twinney agreement, as well as the same payment terms of 2 percent/10, net 30, FOB Coral's warehouse. G & I also offered several additional advantages.

The first benefit was the cost of the product. As illustrated in Exhibit 1, G & I undercut the price Twinney was offering on all three products. This cost differential was made even more attractive by the fact that the prices quoted were for 7-ounce bottles of regular and fragranced product and 3-ounce trial-sized bottles. The leading national brand was offered in similar sizes. The existing agreement with Twinney called for the production of smaller 6-ounce and 2-ounce bottles. Coral's retail selling price was $1.49 for the regular and fragranced shampoo and $0.89 for a trial-size bottle. Shirley believed this was an excellent opportunity to pass on more value to the consumer.

The second advantage was G & I's shipping flexibility. Under the terms of the proposed agreement, the company offered next-day delivery service with no minimum order quantity. G & I was able to offer such favorable terms because its manufacturing facility was located near Coral's central warehouse.

Shirley believed this was an opportunity to support a small local company. If Coral agreed to source its dandruff shampoo from G & I, the account would be one of G & I's largest. In a recent tour of the G & I plant, Shirley was impressed by the cleanliness of its manufacturing facilities; however, she could not help comparing the relatively small-scale operation to Twinney's large shampoo factory.

SHIRLEY'S RECOMMENDATION

Shirley had discussed the dandruff shampoo sourcing issue with the vice president of purchasing in December and knew he was expecting a recommendation from her at the January 25, 2001 meeting at 3 p.m. She was well aware that Coral Drugs had a reputation for long-term relationships with its private-label product suppliers. She was, therefore, still unsure about which supplier to recommend for Coral Dandruff Shampoo.

Exhibit 1
CORAL DRUGS
Price And Size Comparison For Coral Dandruff Shampoo

	Size	*Twinney*	*Size*	*Gorman & Irizawa*
Regular	6 oz.	0.72	7 oz.	0.70
Fragrance	6 oz.	0.85	7 oz.	0.75
Trial	2 oz.	0.47	3 oz.	0.35

Appendix 3

Appendix 3
SAMPLE PRELIMINARY TEACHING NOTE

Richard Ivey School of Business
The University of Western Ontario

IVEY

CASE WRITING WORKSHOP

CORAL DRUGS
PRELIMINARY TEACHING NOTE

CASE SYNOPSIS

Shirley Black glanced at her watch. It was 1 p.m. on January 25, 2001 and only two hours remained before her meeting about Coral Dandruff Shampoo with the vice president of purchasing. As merchandise group coordinator at Coral's head office in Columbus, Ohio, Shirley was trying to decide whether to recommend switching from a large shampoo manufacturer to a small local supplier.

TEACHING OBJECTIVES

This case was written for an introductory course in purchasing and supply chain management, but could also be used in a retailing or merchandising course. It gives students a chance to develop their analytical and decision making skills on a relatively straight forward sourcing decision. It is desirable to do both a qualitative and quantitative analysis and reinforce student skills across both.

IMMEDIATE ISSUE

Whether or not to switch from a large distant shampoo manufacturer to a small low cost local producer.

This preliminary teaching note was prepared by Glen Luinenberg and Professor Michiel R. Leenders as an aid to instructors in the classroom use of the case Coral Drugs. This teaching note should not be used in any way that would prejudice the future use of the case.

Ivey Management Services prohibits any form of reproduction, storage or transmittal without its written permission. This material is not covered under authorization from CanCopy or any reproduction rights organization. To order copies or request permission to reproduce materials, contact Ivey Publishing, Ivey Management Services, c/o Richard Ivey School of Business, The University of Western Ontario, London, Ontario, Canada, N6A 3K7; phone (519) 661-3208; fax (519) 661-3882; e-mail cases@ivey.uwo.ca.

Copyright © 2001, Ivey Management Services　　　　　　　　　　Version 2001-01-18

BASIC ISSUES

1. Supplier selection
2. Supplier relationships
3. Inventory management and logistics
4. Improving customer value

SUGGESTED STUDENT ASSIGNMENT

If you were in the position of Shirley Black, what would you recommend to the vice president of purchasing? Why?

CASE ANALYSIS

The student will probably look at the numbers initially to see just how much Coral will save by going with Gorman and Irizawa. The numbers should come out as follows:

QUANTITATIVE

Assumptions:

i. Each of the three products will sell 20,000 units annually.
ii. Coral will not increase the price on the larger sized bottles G & I will supply (an important assumption).
iii. The increased contribution from the three products taken from Exhibit 1 are:

Regular	$0.02
Fragranced	$0.10
Trial	$0.12

The incremental contribution the product will offer is calculated as follows:

Regular	$0.02 x 20,000 units =	$ 400.00
Fragranced	$0.10 x 20,000 units =	$2000.00
Trial	$0.12 x 20,000 units =	$2400.00
Total		$4800.00

Also, figure out the inventory carrying cost savings. This number proves to be small.

Appendix 3

Assumptions:

i. Average inventory of each product will be 2,000 units.
ii. The monthly inventory carrying cost is 2%.
iii. Inventory value is determined by multiplying Coral's cost (Exhibit 1) by the average inventory (2,000 units per product).
iv. The inventory carrying cost of sourcing the product from G & I is immaterial.

The inventory carrying cost savings is calculated as follows:

Cost of Inventory

Regular	2,000 units x .70 =	$1440.00
Fragranced	2,000 units x .75 =	$1700.00
Trial	2,000 units x .35 =	$ 940.00
Total Investment		$4080.00

Monthly Inventory Carrying Cost = $4080 x .02 = $81.60

Annual Inventory Carrying Cost = $81.60 x 12 = $979.20

Therefore, the total annual savings of going with Gorman and Irizawa is approximately $6,000.00.

QUALITATIVE

When the students push the numbers, they will soon realize that the savings are not large for this product line now. It is hoped that they then focus on the qualitative aspects of the decision. There are advantages and disadvantages of going with either supplier.

Comparison:

Twinney Inc.

> *Advantages*
> - had no problems with service to date
> - larger company that carried a lot of private label products
> - tried and tested formulation
> - stronger research and development
> - stronger financial backing
> - developed a relationship with the company

Disadvantages
- can only order full skids of approximately 4000 units (assume 2% month carrying cost)
- cost
- 3-4 week lead time

G & I

Advantages
- cost
- next day delivery
- any quantity (no minimum order quantity)
- local company (support local jobs)

Disadvantages
- smaller size
- no proven track record
- start again with everything (8 weeks)
- weaker financially

Similarities Between A and B

- payment terms 2% 10, net 30
- FOB warehouse
- responsibilities

Coral risks losing some of its good reputation with its private label suppliers in order to obtain some short-term profitability and convenience. Whether G & I will be around in the long term is a key question.

Presumably, other products could be added to the package to make the total deal and future volume with G & I more meaningful in the future.

It is rather fortuitous that the injection mold has just broken down and new artwork is required also. On a relatively small volume product like this one (total annual volume of about $36,000) testing of a new supplier is not a super high risk. If G & I can handle this order well, they may represent an interesting local option for additional business.

Whether a contract exists in written form with Twinney or not is really not the issue. Under the circumstances, where the supplier generates the artwork, designs the packaging, and may make special investments in equipment, the expectation would normally be that the contract is for a longer term. If Twinney is a large firm, the loss of about $40,000 worth of business is not going to be disastrous. It is, nevertheless, understandable that they would have a minimum lot size of a skid full. And one would expect that minimum lot sizes, shipping quantities, and lead times be agreed to as part of the buyer-supplier understanding.

If Shirley believes that Twinney is unresponsive, perhaps she selected the wrong supplier (a large volume supplier) for the kind of need she has (small volume). In that context, she has an opportunity to correct the situation now. Small local suppliers are generally preferred for small local needs. If $36,000 a year is a big order for G & I, Shirley should weigh the business risk of dealing with such a small supplier and be very careful about this company's viability.

The case does not indicate whether Coral is currently purchasing other products from Twinney or G & I. In this business one would expect that supplier rationalization and direct shipping to the stores might have significant benefits. How much warehousing Coral should be involved in is an interesting question, but no case data are available on this point.

Appendix 4

MAJOR CASE DISTRIBUTION CENTRES OF THE WORLD

The European Case Clearing House
at Cranfield University   Tel: +44 (0)1234 750903
Wharley End, Bedford   Fax: +44 (0)1234 751125
MK43 0JR England
E-mail: **ECCH@cranfield.ac.uk**
Web site: **http://www.ecch.cranfield.ac.uk/**

at Babson College   Tel: +1 781 239 5884
Babson Park,   Fax: +1 781 239 5885
Wellesly, MA 02157
USA
E-mail: **ECCH@babson.edu**

ECCH distributes cases from the following major case producing management schools of the world:

Darden Graduate School of Business Administration, USA
Harvard Business School*, USA
John F. Kennedy School of Government, USA
IESE, Spain
IMD, Switzerland
INSEAD, France
London Business School, England
Richard Ivey School of Business, Canada
Cranfield University, England
Stanford University*, USA

* ECCH does not distribute this material in the United States or Canada

Appendix 4 (continued)

Harvard Business School
Harvard Business School Publishing
Customer Service Department   Tel: +1 800 545 7685
60 Harvard Way   + 1 617 495 6117
Boston, MA 02163, USA   Fax: +1 617 495 6985
E-mail: **custserv@hbsp.harvard.edu**
Web site: **http://www.hbsp.harvard.edu/**

(Harvard Business School Publishing also distributes Ivey cases in the US.)

Richard Ivey School of Business
Ivey Publishing   Tel: +1 519 661 3208
Richard Ivey School of Business   +1 800 649 6355
The University of Western Ontario   Fax: +1 519 661 3882
London, Ontario,
Canada, N6A 3K7
E-mail: **cases@ivey.uwo.ca**
Web site: **http://www.ivey.uwo.ca/cases**

(Ivey also distributes Harvard cases and Harvard Business Review reprints in Canada.)

Darden Graduate School of Business Administration
Darden Educational Materials
  Services   Tel: +1 800 246 3367
Darden Graduate School of   +1 804 924 3009
  Business Administration   Fax: +1 804 924 4859
University of Virginia
P.O. Box 6550
Charlottesville, VA 22906-6550, USA
E-mail: **dardencases@virginia.edu**
Web site: **http://www.darden.virginia.edu/**

index

Academic credit for case writing, 158-60
Action trigger, 56, 57, 62-66, 74, 78, 100
Alternatives, 85, 86-87
Appendix(es), 115-16, 122
Apprentice system, 9
Armchair case, 5
Assignment questions, student, 28, 72, 119, 126, 139, 40, 149, 152

Background, general company, 84, 85, 90-91, 100, 112-13, 116, 120

Case(s)
   analysis, 119-20, 139, 140
   armchair, 5
   assignment. See Assignment question, student
   class, 3
   coding, 124
   completion, on-time, 15
   conclusion, 65, 87, 94
   cost, 4, 14, 164, 165-66, 167
   date, 152
   definition, 1, 3-5, 47, 173
   Difficulty Cube. See Case Difficulty Cube
   distribution centers, 134, 136, 184
   draft, 28. See also Rough draft
   editing, 29, 121-28
   features, 33, 37-41
   financing, 164, 165-66
   focus choice(s). See Focus choices, case
   format(s), 4, 21, 36, 170-71. See also Format, case
   formatting, 124
   information. See Information
   information form, 134-135
   international, 166-67
   lead. See Lead
   length, 36, 116-17, 155-56, 169
   life, 156-57
   location, 39, 74, 75, 90
   obsolescence, 8, 32, 156, 157
   origin, 25, 31-41
   outline, 24, 71, 84-87. See also subtitles
   plan. See Case Plan
   popularity, 153. See also Preferences, case
   preferences. See Preferences, case
   quality, 13-14, 24, 25, 26, 28, 160
   quantity, 14. See also Productivity
   reasons for using, 5-7, 47, 173
   reasons for writing, 7-8
   registration, 134-36
   release. See Release
   relevance, 8. See also Information, relevant
   revision. See Revision, case
   sample, 50, 175
   series, 59, 80, 168-69
   Shopping List, 50-55
   source, 4, 5
   story line. See Story line, case
   subtitles, 24, 28, 84-87, 123, 148
   time, 74, 75
   title, 74, 80, 117, 124, 128. See also Title page
   turnover, 156-57
   unreleased, 9, 138
   updating, 157
   writer. See Writer(s), case
   writing. See Writing, case. See also Case writing process
Case Difficulty Cube, 13, 16, 17-24, 33-35, 74, 75, 79, 82, 83, 115, 116, 147, 155
   analytical dimension, 17-19, 34, 75, 82, 83

Index

conceptual dimension, 17, 19-20, 34-35, 82, 83
presentation dimension, 17, 20-21, 35, 82, 83,148, 155
Case Method, 1-3, 5, 6, 47, 69, 72
  purposes, 5-7
  skills developed by, 7
Case Origin Grid, 37-42, 50, 57, 66, 118, 163
Case Plan, 13, 16, 24-25, 53, 54, 55, 71-97, 101, 106, 109, 111-12, 113, 117, 163
  components, 71
  preparation, 26-27
Case Shopping List, 50-52, 53, 54, 55, 57, 163
Case Teaching Plan, 29, 140, 142-44
  agenda, 142, 143
  board plan, 143, 144
  participation plan, 142, 143
  preference list, 142, 143
  time plan, 142, 143
Case writing effectiveness, 13
  challenges to, 13-16
  communication, 15-16
  objectives, 13-15
  tools for, 17-25
Case writing process, 10, 26, 50, 88, 174
  three phases, 25-30
Case writing workshop, 9, 162-63
CD ROM, 4
Christensen, C. Roland, iv
Class test, 4, 29, 144-53
  cause and effect diagram, 149-50
  kinds of, 146
  need for, 145
  results interpretation, 149-51
  revisions after, 144, 145
COLIS, 136
Communication
  supervisor/case writer, 16, 23-24, 72, 163-64
  with contact person(s), 16, 23-24, 29, 72
Conclusion, case, 65, 87, 94

Confidentiality, data, 48, 53, 66, 102, 109, 134, 173
Consulting and case writing, 157-58
Contact person(s), 10. See also Communication, Lead
  background information, 49
  information for, 49, 173
  reasons for cooperating, 48-49
  role, 47, 49, 174
Contact, initial, 25, 31, 44-56. See also Interview, first
  arranging for, 45-46
  definition, 44
  objective, 44
  preparing for, 46-62
Contact, second, 27, 95, 96. See also Interview, subsequent
Conventions, case writing, 113-17, 124-28
  abbreviations, 126
  appendixes, 115-16
  assignment questions, 126
  exhibits, 114-15
  facts, opinions, attributions, 114
  past tense, 114
  referencing, 124
  reprinting, 126
  title page, 124-25
Copeland, Dr., 1
Copyright, 124-25, 130, 152
Cost(s), case writing, 4, 14, 164, 165-66, 167
Course
  content, 33, 38, 40, 41, 50, 51
  outline, 50
  planning, 31-32
  review, 32

Darden Graduate School of Business Administration, 185
Data. See also Information
  coding and sorting, 109-10
  confidentiality. See Confidentiality, data
  numerical, 67-68
  reliability and validity, 106-07

requirements list, 24, 28, 71, 87-94, 99, 100, 101, 109
security, 66, 109
sources, 49, 99
specification, 89
Data collection, 5, 28, 84, 88, 95, 96, 99-110
pitfalls and difficulties, 105-09
Decision frame cut, 57, 60-63, 74, 78, 79, 87, 100, 106
Decision maker, 39, 57, 66, 73-75, 92-93, 152
Definition, case, 1, 3-5, 47, 73
Disclaimer, 124-25, 130
Disguise, 27, 48, 53, 55, 66-70, 74, 79, 89, 96, 122
approach, 69-70
individual names, 67, 68
numerical data, 67-68
objectives, 66-67
organization, name of, 67, 68, 69
other information, 69
reasons for, 67
Donham, Wallace B., 2

ECCH, 134, 136, 184
Editing, case, 29, 121-28
Editing checklist, 121-28
clarity, 122-23, 128
coherence, 123
completeness, 122
conciseness, 122
congruence, 121
consistency, 122, 127
control, 123
conventions, 124-28
correctness, 122, 128
Ethics, case writing, 152, 157-58, 161
Exhibits, 105, 114-15, 122, 148

Film, 4
Focal person, See Decision maker
Focus choices, case, 55, 57-66
decision maker, choice of, 57, 66
issue, choice of, 57
timing, choice of, 57-63

Format, case, 4, 21, 36, 170-71
audio tape, 4
CD ROM, 4
disk, 4, 170-71
film, 4
video tape, 4, 21, 105, 141, 170
written, 4, 21, 170
Fox, W. Sherwood, 2

Gay, Dean, 1

Harvard Business School, 1, 2, 185
Publishing, 136, 185

Information. See also Data
background. See Background, general company
facts vs opinions, 103, 114, 120-21
missing, 6, 20, 21, 28, 29, 36, 83, 120, 145, 147
quotes, 104, 114, 126
referencing, 124
relevant, 20, 21, 28, 83, 89, 91, 113
source(s) of, 49, 99
In-house cases, 169-70
International cases, 166-67
Interview, first, 25, 26, 46-56. See also Contact, initial
beginning, 52-53
conducting, 52-55
ending, 53,55
following, 53, 55-56
guidelines, 52-53
notes, 55-56, 101. See also Note taking
objective, 52
Interview, personal, 99-105
preparation for, 100-101
Interview, subsequent, 27, 101
See also Contact, second
Interview, telephone, 105
Interviewing rules, case, 101-04
Issue(s)
basic, 118, 139-40
choice of, 14, 57

Index

clarity, 74-75
immediate, 118, 139-40
specific, 85, 86, 93-94, 113
urgency of, 64-65, 78
Ivey. See Richard Ivey School of Business
Ivey Publishing, 136, 185

Lead, 10, 25, 31, 42-44
definition, 42
types of, 42-43
ways of finding, 43-44
Learning with cases, 2, 6
Learning objectives. See Objectives, educational
Length, case, 36, 116-17, 155-56, 169
Location of organization, 39, 74-75, 90

Missing information. See Information, missing
Morrow, Ellis H., 2
Multimedia case(s), 170-71

Neville, K. P. R., 2
Note taking, 104. See also Interview, notes

Obsolescence, case, 8, 32, 156, 157
Objectives, educational, 13-14, 15, 16, 21, 24, 31, 33-35, 37, 59, 87, 88, 116, 139, 146, 147. See also Teaching objectives
Opening paragraph, 24, 71-82, 84, 85, 117-18
checklist, 73-82, 117
Organization, case. See Outline, case
Origin, case, 25, 31-41
Outline, case, 24, 71, 84-87. See also Subtitles

Photographs, 105, 141
Plan, case. See Case Plan
Preferences, case, 33, 35-36, 37-42, 43, 44, 50-52, 54, 57, 66

Productivity, 14, 163, 165

Quality, case, 13-14, 24, 25, 26, 28, 160
Quantity, case, 14
Quotes, 104, 114, 126

Recording, 104-05
Reading(s), 3, 6, 115, 140, 141
Release, 4, 5, 25, 27, 29, 45, 46, 95, 96, 129-38, 145, 173
delayed, 137
form, 16, 48, 131-32, 134
kinds, 136-37
multiple, 136
non-, 9, 138
not required, 137-38
purposes, 129-30
request, 131, 133
restricted, 136
tasks, 4, 130-36
traditional, 136
Release, provisional, 24, 25, 27, 88, 95-97
Relevance, case, 8
Re-release, 28, 29, 30, 137, 145, 151, 157
Research case(s), 169
Revision, case, 29, 151-53, 157. See also Rough draft, revision.
Richard Ivey School of Business, 2, 9, 134, 162, 185
Rough draft, 111-17
revision, 120-21
Rough draft conventions, 113-17
appendixes, 115-16
exhibits, 114-15
facts, opinions, attributions, 114
past tense, 114

Samples, 105, 141
Security, data, 66, 109
Series, case, 59, 80, 168-69
Source, case, 4, 5,
Story line, case, 47, 58, 66, 100, 111, 112, 113, 122

cut, 57-63, 74, 76-78, 106
Student as case writer. See Writer(s), case, student(s)
Student preferences. See Preferences, case
Subtitles, 24, 28, 84-87, 123, 148

Teaching aids, 105, 140, 141
Teaching objectives, 4, 24, 28, 83, 87, 113, 115, 118, 139-40, 155-56. See also Objectives, educational
   brief statement of, 71, 82-84
Teaching note, 29-30, 95, 139-44
   headings, 139-40
   purpose, 139
Teaching note, preliminary, 28, 117-20, 131, 139, 179
Terminology, 10-11
Theory(ies), 6, 19-20, 32, 33-35, 38, 41, 47, 50, 147
Time, case, 74, 75
Time, case writing process, 174
Time plan, 24, 71, 94-95, 140
Timing of issue, 57-66
   decision frame cut, 57, 60-63
   story line cut, 57-60, 62
Title page, 124-25, 130
   copyright, 124-25, 130
   disclaimer, 124-25, 130
   sample, 125
Towl, Andrew R., iv

University of Western Ontario, 2. See also Richard Ivey School of Business

Video tape, 4, 21, 105, 141, 170
Videotaping, 104-05
Visitors to class, 141, 146

Workshop. See Case Writing Workshop
Writer(s,) case, 9, 10, 161
   assistant(s), research, 9, 10, 161
   associate(s), research, 10, 161

full-time, 9
judgment(s), personal, 120
productivity, 14, 163, 165
role, 47-48, 49, 102, 108, 157-58, 174
selection of, 161-62
student(s), 9, 10, 161, 162, 164-65
supervision, 163-64
training, 9, 162-63
Writing, case, 95, 111-28
   academic credit, 158-60
   ethics, 152, 157-58, 161
   reasons for, 31-33
   rough draft, 111-17
   skills, 161